SPOKEN SOL

A Way With Words

Spoken Sol: A Way With Words
ISBN: 979-8-234-03917-0
Published by: S.O.L. Centre LLC

Printed in the United States of America

All real-life anecdotes are told with permission from actual parties involved and recorded to the best of the author's recollection. Names in some instances have not been used at the request of the individuals referenced. In some cases, parties mentioned are deceased. Details of some instances have been slightly modified to enhance readability, or to ensure privacy. Any resemblance of any other parties is purely coincidental.

DEDICATION

To lovers who love love.

FOREWORD

"The true measure of a man isn't how he carries himself when everything is going well, it's more about how he handles adversity. How he responds when he's knocked down. Does he lie there and stay down, or does he dust himself off and get back up?

Sol has gotten back up and exemplifies the true measure of a man. Youth incarceration has held many a man down, rendered them helpless and hopeless to get back up, but not Sol.

Sol chose to make his trials and tribulations his fuel that motivates his comeback and what a comeback it has been. Whether it's art, poetry, massage therapy, or being one of the top stylists; he pursues excellence that shows in his work. Each painting, each poem, each massage, and each cut is done with meticulous attention to detail, creativity, and authenticity, which are also all strong characteristics that make Sol uniquely and authentically who he is. That is why Sol sharing his journey resonates with all those who hear his story and serves as an inspiration to many.

Michael Perry BA; MPA

FROM THE AUTHOR

This book is the product of self-reflection, personal studies and therapy. It is written with the intention of understanding the human condition. The best way for me to absorb knowledge is to share it whether through journaling, intimate conversations or love letters. This piece is a compilation of them all. The result is Spoken Sol – an intellectual journey where wordsmith meets enlightenment, and poetic prose solicits healing. Each page is intended to be a conversation piece and each conversation bring us closer.

Love and light,
Sol Amen-Ra

CONTENTS

Spoken Sol: A Way With Words

The Biggest Challenge

People often ask me what the biggest challenge was after coming home from prison. What was it like to come home after serving a life sentence?

Not to sound arrogant but there weren't any challenges when I came home in terms of rebuilding my life. The challenge was being incarcerated and making up my mind about the path I was going to take to reach success despite the circumstances around me. The challenge was being able to realistically visualize my future. Coming home was a matter of application.

I came home and built my business and established my brand. There was no other option. I wouldn't let there be. I was fueled by nay sayers. I was fueled by the people who placed me in the box of being a prison intellectual...the brother who goes to jail and has nothing else to do but read and gains a mastery of the King's English. As if prison is a peaceful library minus the threat of killers, gangs, and racist officers who have the protection of a "man down" button.

It's been almost 10 years now and I've realized a challenge that I want to share. The challenge is relationship. I grew up hustling. Our primary motive was to take care of family and impress the ladies with the spoils of our labor. Courtship was a big part of our lives. I came home to a society that doesn't honor the courtship process. I listen to homies who would tell me they were going to smoke loud with a female and that was considered fore play. That was the exchange. In the online dating scene, I kept hearing about this phrase

"Netflix and chill". That was courting. Strange. I'm a courtier. I truly enjoy the process of relating and getting to know a woman. I bumped into another challenge. A language barrier. I'd arrange a casual meet and greet with a woman just to see how the conversation flowed and to make sure she looked like her picture. These "meet and greets" were translated as "dates". In my mind, a date is when I pick you up, open doors, and plan an evening around mutual interest and fun activities.

Now my challenge is to accept this new world as reality... I cannot.

January 10, 2019 - Priceless

My village Elder is "Paw Paw". Tribe leader. Charismatic friend. The Michael Jordan of men. When you see his image, you can hear Frankie Beverly in the background. His image spoke to me this morning.

He was extremely polished and very particular about his grooming needs. His taper...His beard…The circumference of his Afro. Only a few barbers have cut his hair. I am one of them. I say that with pride.

Before I had Jesus, I had Paw Paw. He took care of me in a way that no invisible deity could. I was a young player with daddy issues. I vowed to never be like my lame-ass dad. Then I became a dad and became him. He was lame because he was absent. My daughter was conceived and I went to prison. I became him. Not being present for your seed is lame. This man was present. He was there for my daughter while I was away. That reality provided me the mental space to serve time and build my character. Otherwise, the guilt would've swallowed me. The peace of mind he gave me allowed me to forgive my own dad for being absent. You can't judge what you are. To condemn him was to condemn myself. I was already locked up. Why would I incarcerate myself again? Not. I survived. I prevailed. I became free.

Free from prison. Free from mental chains. Free from generational curses.

Because of him.

There was no way to repay him. He took care of the village and his wife took care of him. They were complete. Nothing missing. Nothing needed.

Very... Particular...about his grooming.

He would come to me and close his eyes. He trusted me with his image.
Priceless.

January 21, 2019

I was leaving San Diego for LA. We passed thru San Clemente and I took this shot. It spoke to me. Thus...Spoken Sol.

I shared it with my friend. She's a spiritual chic. She asked what moved me to take it. I explained I was hit with a sense of complete gratitude. I philosophized about my journey in my mind and was hit with the moment. I looked at all the things that weren't ideal about my travels. But a part of me that likes to cut thru the BS to get to the bottom line.

Are you here?

Yes.

Are you healthy?

Yes.

Are you capable?

Yes.

Well STFU and make it happen.

Then I felt a sense of overwhelming gratitude. The Sun grabbed my complete attention and I took the photo.

She said "Woooow!" in a way that didn't make sense to me. I asked her to explain. She said God sent you an angel in that moment!

Huh?

She said, "Look at the sun."

Ok.

"Do you see the sun ray...the single friggin' ray! There should be many but there's only one."

Ooooo...K...

"Now look at the bottom of the ray. There's an orb...an angel sent directly to you. Wow Sol."

I hadn't even noticed any of that. For me it was a moment.

So I share it because that is the premise of my page. Spoken Sol.

Right now I'm inside a leap of faith. I have seen signs and wonders. I'm on the right path and I know it even if my current circumstance isn't ideal. No one leaps in comfort. If there is no risk, there is no leap. I can't imagine life without a dream. A dream comes with struggle and perseverance. You have to see the outcome in spite of the circumstance. You have to be a student of manifestation. That requires humility. With humility comes grace.

I claim what's mine...even before I see it.

- Spoken Sol

February 9, 2019

A healthy stroke of the ego can easily feel like love. However, it is only a stroke of the ego. And love can easily feel like something divine. But it is only an emotion.

I could argue that all emotions are divine. I could further argue that hate is the most influential of them all. People are motivated by hate. It's a mobilizing force. In contrast, we roll our eyes at lovers.

We encounter two people about to fight and we pull out cell phones to record it. We witness two lovers expressing their affection in public and we demonize it. "They need to get a room!"

Why is that?

Why does hate deserve an audience and love deserve a room?

Strange Americans.

February 12, 2019

My new friend Ben lives on the streets of San Diego. I snapped a picture of him with a smile. I greeted him and we talked. I was impressed by the honesty of his petition and the spirit in which he presented it. He wasn't begging. He was asking for assistance. All he wanted was some weed and a van. That was his ambition.

I realized that Ben wasn't homeless. He was so "at home" with himself that all he wanted was the freedom to drive around and make "home" wherever he chose to park.

That's pretty groovy.

He wasn't the type of homeless guy you could easily ignore. He grabs your attention and gives you a smile.
It's amazing that in a city of such wealth, there is such homelessness.

It's amazing that such wealth can be found in the presence of the homeless.

- Humbled Soul

February 22, 2019

The path of the healer isn't always fun. The nurse who loses a patient... The mentor who loses a youth to the system... The lover who heals the beloved only to witness them walk away.

A healer is created to heal. A healer heals. That's their purpose and function. A healer cannot have an emotional investment in a particular outcome. The healer arrives with a light that is meant to be given away, a love that has to be shared. Wellness is the outcome. Wellness is the intent and the result.

Empaths wrestle with this reality. But a nurse can't be mad at the patient for dying. A mentor can't be mad that the youth who slipped away. A lover can't be mad when the beloved makes a choice that doesn't involve them. It is simply the path of the healer. You show up. You love. You heal.

That is all.

February 22, 2019

Impressed by the substance of her conversation I had to ask the typical question "Why are you single?".

"Men, can't handle me." Spoken without pause.

"Why?" I responded.

"I'm too much." She said with a slight grin.

"Why?" I pressed.

"What do you mean?" As if she really didn't understand.

I mean...

> "You don't seem to want to be single...but you are. By choice. Because you are TOO MUCH. I get it. I'm asking why? Why is that your story? Why do you want to be 'too much' knowing it's the reason for your singleness?"

"I'm ok with being alone! I'm not dumbing myself down just to have a man."

"I'm not suggesting that you should. I'm observing that you are easy to talk to and easy to be around, so obviously you can maintain your TOO MUCHNESS and still enjoy the company of a man. Yes? Unless you aren't as cool as you seem...Maybe I just caught you off guard.

Or...

Maybe this is really you. Sweet, fun, engaging. Maybe you don't need a man to handle you. Maybe you just need a man to be present while you handle yourself."

-Spoken Sol

March 7, 2019 - The View

I was going thru a thing. You know... entertaining darkness. Negative thoughts. Focusing on the things that I don't have. Seeing my victory somewhere in the distant future. I sank into that place where we criticize ourselves relentlessly and revisit the emotions of past mistakes. In these moments I like to be extreme. I like to dive in and meet the bullshit head on. Prison teaches you how to use fear as a weapon against chaos. So when Darkness and his friends (negativity and lack) surround me, I stand as a lion amongst wolves.

I was going thru a thing. You know... looking at life the wrong way. Negative thoughts. I was looking at the things that I don't have. I was overlooking myself. Not seeing the blessing that I am. I came back to myself, took three deep breaths, and opened my eyes.

I saw this view. I was totally present with this view.

I thought to myself... "What type of man has this view?"

I answered myself... "You"

The darkness instantly disappeared. Light illuminated my soul. A treasure of gifts was inside of me. I grabbed one and hit the block (went to the marketplace).

Moral to story: Life is in the view. God made you matter. You make it happen. Whatever "it" is. View it the right way. There is power in perception.

March 25, 2019 - (Dear Self)

Dear Self,

When you are a dream chaser possessed by a healthy amount of ambition you are bound to suffer setbacks. Pauses of motion. Decline. The bigger picture will seem out of reach. Frustration will visit you. Don't deny he's at the door. Don't duck him. Answer the door with grace and politely decline his invitation to go grab a drink. No need to socialize and get your mind off things. Life is urgent. A breakthrough is near. That's why he's here seeking to distract you.

You've felt this feeling before. You had to visualize freedom from the infinite darkness of a jail cell. You fought the justice system in handcuffs. You have suffered the deepest of legal setbacks. You are built to withstand pressure. And when you fight, you win. Give yourself credit. Don't trip.

You are not at a disadvantage. You have God and the greatest of human values, health. What a nice place to begin when you think you have nothing. Added to that is your ability to visualize the future and manifest your dreams. You have created your life, literally, from the substance of your imagination. God put a current inside of you that becomes currency. Wherever you show up, you bring value. You have the power to make moves without thinking about money, so don't let thinking about money take your power away. Can you dig it...

Count blessings and give credit where it is due. Starting with you.

May 17, 2019

When frustrated and overcome with life they say..."I can't see the forest for the trees." But if you raise your consciousness...not only can you see above the trees that compose the forest... you can see far beyond to the mountains that may become your next challenge.

Look at the big picture. See how beautiful it is. Appreciate every aspect and bask in the wonders of God's creation. Some of us are meant to rise to the top. We were created to be special. That means we are bound to rise above. No great view comes without great challenge. It's ok. Embrace it.

You might lose family along the way and friends might become haters. Lovers may morph into strangers. But it doesn't matter because when you embrace yourself as called, destined, chosen...the angels become your companions.

Dome thoughts.

May 18, 2019 - Message from a Palm Tree

I was leaving the beach after meditating in the sun. I saw this tree and it reminded me of a conversation that I had with my coworkers. My coworkers are beautiful women. Stylists.

I sat in the break room listening to them talk about what they wanted to change about themselves. They were talking about Botox and plastic surgery. I looked up to see, specifically, what they were talking about. A stunning, young blond was talking about her eyes. Wrinkles around her eyes. Another stunning middle eastern female chimed in about her lips. Injections. Fillers. A curvy, eye-catching Latina, chimed in about her weight. Losing pounds. She was quintessentially "thick". Perfect as is.

I shook my head and laughed to myself. They asked why. I chose not to comment because I'm not a woman. I wasn't raised in an image driven culture where you can be absolutely stunning yet still feel like something is missing.

Thus, the palm tree. The thick, short, palm tree.

I'm new to California so I appreciate details that the natives might take for granted. I'm used to seeing tall, slim, palm trees that sway with the wind. Seeing a short, stubby, palm tree caught my eye. It stood out in appearance and location. It was growing from sand, chilling on the beach. Grounded in itself providing a forefront to a beautiful backdrop for anyone with eyes and an appreciation for beauty.

Funny... All my coworkers who complained had relationship issues. Witnessing this palm tree made me wonder if their issues stemmed from their relationship with themselves. I imagine being a 30-year young, beautiful woman, with a perfect body. Gainfully employed, intelligent, and successful. Yet plagued by anxiety over crow's feet. Crow's feet are the imprint left by a smile. What a dilemma.

-Message from a Palm Tree

May 20, 2019 - Moon Goddess

She was a glaring light amongst darkness. She was a moon goddess, but she didn't know who she was. Somewhere along the way someone told her she was a dry, crusty, barren, worthless, rock. Lost in space. That was the darkness that surrounded her and composed the background for her shine. But she couldn't see it because she had grown to believe the narrative that was handed to her by unhealthy experiences with men.

She grew to trust my conversation.

She said "You're different. How is it possible that you see me so clearly and you barely even know me?"

"We are from the same space. I am a reflection of the same light that makes you shine so bright." But she couldn't see herself as radiant. Her darkness had become so dense that she couldn't see her connection to Source. Thus, she had no idea that she controlled the tide.

We talked about her relationships with men. She said that she wanted to find a man who would see beyond her drag, her appearance. She wore make up that announced she was either a make-up artist or a performer. In truth, she was both. She made herself impossible to see beyond. Her presence came with a sense of awe.

To the primitive mind she inspired a host of dark fantasies. To the evolved mind she inspired an intense desire to heal.

I saw her clearly. Her make up was really war paint. She was fighting demons and resisting angels. She didn't know who she could trust. Her lack of trust made room for the dark clouds of uncertainty.

I reminded her: The darkness that surrounds you also serves as the background to your shine. What do you want to do with your stage? What story do you want to tell?

What's the narrative of your existence?

Moral to story...Once you know your source, you become a force. You control the tide. Life doesn't happen to you. You happen to it.

July 2, 2019

The bad part about breaking up with me is that I'm not prone to express resistance. Which will make you think that I don't care. The pain of saying goodbye will be amplified by my lack of concern for your absence. This is where my spirituality becomes painful. I have no desire to control anyone's feelings or choices. I believe in freedom.

When you first met me, you described me as the most present man you'd ever met. That's true today. I'm present... even when you leave, I'm present. For me, it's not a matter of missing you because I appreciated every second we shared. I valued every moment. My heart is built to wish you the best even if I am not involved. This is where my spirituality becomes painful. I can love you as a lover. I can love you as a friend. I can love you as a memory. When love is fluid there can be no hard feelings.

Even when the moon says goodbye.

July 2, 2019

She was venting to the wrong person...Me. She told me about her x boyfriend. She called him a narcissist. She told me stories of how he tried to play her. She awaited my response.

I told her the best way to avoid a narcissist is not to be one.

She became offended. She suggested that I was victim blaming. The problem with her assessment is that I don't believe in victims. There are only volunteers.

So, when looking at the energy of a narcissist I immediately look at its reflection. I ask, "What is it about you that seeks his brand of attention?" "Have you ever weaponized your empathy?" "Have you ever thought that your empathetic love would change a man's perception?" Like, maybe if you love him the right way, he'll see you as The One?

She became irritated and told me about all the lies he told her. She painted herself as the victim. "He used me! He played me!!"

I asked "What did God create you for? What purpose did He intend for you to serve?" She couldn't answer.

I concluded that a lack of spirituality is the root of victimhood. For if you have a sense of spirituality, you understand yourself as a vehicle of God...an instrument to be played. With spirituality you have power over your ability to serve. It's why nurses heal, why evangelists go on missions, why volunteers give their time to the less fortunate. The God aspect makes us derive great pleasure from serving. If you play a spiritual person music will be the result, dance will be the response. Not pain and suffering.

My humble observation.

July 5, 2019

Tonight, we are going to role-play.

I'm going to pretend that I don't know where your G spot lives. I'm going to act as if I don't know the difference between giving you a climax or giving you an orgasm.

Tonight, I'm going to forget my intimacy issues and hold your hand as we kiss. Tonight, your hands will be my mentor. I will watch you touch yourself. Touch yourself as if I'm not in the room. My tongue will soon follow the instructions of your fingers.

Tonight, your body will be a temple. I will bow to you. I will kneel before your sacred space. The place where you give birth to life. I will listen for God.

"Oh God, yes!"

Once I hear God's name, I will know I have arrived. I will want you to arrive as well. I will want you to come.

"I'm coming…"

Tonight, we are going to role-play.

I'm going to summons the thirst of a prophet who walked 40 days and 40 nights thru a desert, but I will not desert you. I will make you, my oasis. I will drink your sweet nectar and consume your flesh. Tonight, we will have communion.

Tonight, you will be my virgin and I will be your Holy Spirit. I will give you my seed without touching you.

Tonight, we are going to role-play. You will be the savior and I will be the Roman soldier. I'm going to beat you with my tongue and stab you with my sword. I'm going to open the windows and make you a public sacrifice. I want the world to see you arch your back as you rise again for the second coming.

Tonight...we will have all night...

To role play.

July 5, 2019 - Untitled

She clung to him as if he was life. Breathing him deeply.

She'd bask in his light as if he was the sun. He was the very source of her vitamin D.

She needed him in order to feel well. As a rainy day stimulates depression, his radiance was something of an existential aphrodisiac. It not only made her feel alive, it turned her on.

She was crazy about him. Nothing about their relationship made sense. It wasn't intellectual. It was a feeling. A spiritual suspicion. An impulse. She felt born to serve him.

She had given herself to many men. She had given her heart, her mind, her body, and her capabilities. She had sacrificed her needs to make it work. She understood defeat. Her failed marriage was a symbol of this reality. Yet, something about him inspired her to serve. She couldn't help it. Even when her mind tried to hold her back her spirit persisted, sensing the danger of deliverance.

He opened her up and let her go. Like a sunray to the fragrance of an obedient rose. He was incapable of taking her personal. Yet, she needed to be taken, claimed, owned.

Her love statement was "Take me home and put me in a vase. “In his mind, such an action would deprive her of the life she was meant to live.

They spoke two different languages. He didn't understand that she belonged to him. She didn't understand that he belonged to God.

July 10, 2019

I didn't mean to ghost you. It wasn't intentional. The attraction was real. Our connection was real. Truth is, I've become seduced by social media and dating apps. When I look at my phone throughout the day I have a 10-minute window. I check messages and texts. I check out posts from friends.

I logged on to read your message and was faced with the opportunity to swipe right on a pretty face. It has become an unconscious habit. I swipe a few times before I check messages.

I read your message but I have messages from other women I was communicating with before you. I respond to your message. I respond to theirs. One of which I'm exchanging numbers with because we're going to meet soon.

This is the issue with social media. It becomes an unconscious response. I wasn't playing a game. It wasn't my intention to chat with you only to discard you. I was sincerely getting to know you. But I was sincerely getting to know other women as well. That's how it happens on both sides. Male and female. I apologize for allowing you to get caught up in the shuffle.

It has happened to me as well but I didn't take it personally. I don't assume that I'm for everybody. I don't assume everybody is for me. If a woman, suddenly, stops communicating I assume she's found what she was looking for. It wasn't me.

But I know your heart is built different. You might think something better came along or you weren't enough. That's not the case.

Pardon me for being rude. Forgive me for any damage I've done to your faith.

July 26, 2019 - Strange Americans

Truth hurts... and I admit that I hurt her deeply. She was older than me. I thought she was seasoned, ripe, mature. But she was a lil girl trapped in a childhood trauma. Added to that, her husband left her. She had abandonment issues. I loved her. In the moment. She wanted that moment to last forever but our differences were too strong. I was moving on and she was holding on.

I hurt her.

She demonized me to her friends while we were doing the back-and-forth thing. Trying to maintain our friendship while releasing the relationship.

I asked her to keep our business between us. But she was prone to drama, gossip, girl talk. Her friends started following my page trying to gather information. Trying to figure me out. Then one of them in-boxed me. She called herself defending her friends honor, but really, she just wanted some attention.

I entertained her.

She couldn't wait to tell me all the things that were shared about me. I suggested that we meet in person to talk. She accepted.

I could've taken the scenario wherever I wanted to at this point. I knew that she was one of the main characters speaking against my name. Part of me wanted to transgress with her for my own selfish fulfillment. But I didn't. I withheld myself. Simply to demonstrate character rather than exact revenge. Now she has to live with the guilt of knowing she'd betray her friend, or perhaps she has no guilt at all. Either way... My character stands "mess" free.

Strange Americans.

July 30, 2019

She invited me into her private space. She welcomed me into her home. This picture was on her wall. It was my first impression of who she was to herself. Privately. It held me captive for a moment.

Meeting someone in public is one thing. Entering someone's home is another. Home is where you rest your soul and remove your social mask. She was a powerful woman in a gated community. Secure. Bold. Professional. She controlled who had access to her presence. Which is why being invited into her home was a big deal. She was a calculated woman. Shrewd. Measured.

When I first met her, it was in a cigar lounge. Her friend was the owner. The same friend was disguised as a server. I was being observed and didn't know. I was being "checked out". Usually, I'm extremely conscious of my surroundings, but this space, a cave of sorts, had a speak-easy vibe. It felt like a social club where only certain individuals belonged. I felt home. Added to the chill atmosphere was her presence. Bold and beautiful. She was a virago. Her posture released the fragrance of victory. You could tell that she had been thru some shit. Her mannerisms radiated from inner conviction. She was sure of who she was. Which made her, not only, attractive...but magnetic.

Upon stepping inside of her private space, I was greeted by this image. An image that reflected her soul. No connection is more honest that when two souls agree upon art. She instantly became someone who I wanted to paint with words.

Some women remind you of love songs. But her presence reminded you of the theme music for James Bond.

August 27, 2019

I entered an unfamiliar bar fully prepared to honor my PTSD by positioning myself with my back to the wall so I could see everything going on. It didn't happen. I sat down at the bar with no thought of anything but the atmosphere I had walked into. I took in the art, the signs, the pictures on the wall. This image spoke to me. I later found that it was a picture of the owner. I don't know why I was so taken by the image of a woman smoking a cigar. Perhaps because California women don't tend to smoke. However she was European. She spoke with a heavy accent and had the spirit of a female Gangsta. She was a boss.

As we talked, I couldn't help but feel like I was talking to two different people. Her spirit was extremely feminine but her views were feminist. She was barely 30 years old but she possessed a veteran mentality. She was a student of power. Women like her have been thru extreme circumstances that create extreme convictions. She walked the world with a 'certainty of self' which made her beyond beautiful.

The wedding ring on her finger was more of a statement than a symbol of love. It looked like something a wealthy man would give a trophy wife. Enough bling to silence her during his indiscretions. A flamboyant reminder of what she would be missing if she ever left him. But she wasn't the type of woman who could be impressed or oppressed by a man's wealth. She divorced him, kept the ring, but wore it on a different finger. She wasn't the type of woman to allow emotions to cloud her judgment. If there was a loss there was a lesson. Her personal evolution was the premiere value of her existence. You could build her but not destroy her. Thus was the statement of her presence. She was pro woman, pro power, professional. A boss.

September 6, 2019 - Special

She was a special friend. One of those people you meet and have an instant connection with. I loved her and I told her so. Way before using that type of language was warranted. Our connection was that strong. She understood where I was coming from because she was coming from the same place. We, somehow, summoned each other into our lives energetically. She was perfectly flawed. I was flawed perfectly. Together, we were a force to be reckoned with.

We didn't last.

The relationship wasn't built to last. I came into her life simply to remind her that love was possible. Before me, she was on the fence about relationships. I awakened her heart and she gave it to another man. The challenge of unconditional love is to applaud the beloved's choice to move on. The challenge of unconditional love is to be able to give the gift of goodbye.

I let her go. I saluted her man and blessed their new relationship. But randomly I'd get a message from her. In those moments I knew that there was trouble in paradise. She would only reach out to me when things weren't going well with him. The challenge of unconditional love is to love without conditions. There was not a condition that would prevent me from loving her. And sometimes loving her meant leaving her alone.

September 7, 2019 - BigSexy

BigSexy is a perfect description for her. She's larger than the average woman. Her full figure is adorned with rolls, muffin tops, and cellulite, but she carries herself like a model. Her style stands out. She smells like a rose. Her make up is always on point. Her style is one of a kind. She doesn't walk the world seeking to be skinny. She embraces her size and carries it well. Her insecurities only amplify her sense of style like blindness amplifies the sense of sound. When she is present, you notice. She attracts attention. Her "ok-ness with self" makes her sexy. She's more than a woman. She comes with theme music. And good music makes you want to dance.

Shout out to my BigSexies out there.

September 11, 2019 - Fast

She was what my wise mother would describe as "Fast". Pronounced "Fass". She was far too young to be so sexually aware. Her presence exuded womanhood. She knew how to smile. She knew how to use her eyes as weapons in conversation. She understood her power.

She had been sexually abused by older family members. Her 'cry out' fell on deaf ears, so she learned how to use herself to defend herself. She understood men from the perspective of a sexualized little girl. She understood men as predators who were always lurking for an opportunity to catch her alone. She often questioned why they focused on her instead of the other lil girls. Why her? She wasn't as pretty as them. She wasn't as developed. Yet she always seemed to be the center of their attention.

There was a power inside of her and she learned how to use it. She wasn't the type of girl who could roam the world as anyone's victim. She learned the game and got good at it. To the point, she grew to resent men for being so weak. She became the abuser. Using her sexuality as a weapon she reclaimed her power in the inevitable, secret, exchanges.

Being dominant became the signature of her character. She was young, wise, and shrewd. Her friends looked to her for relationship advice. She was a natural leader because she inherited the responsibility of fighting monsters at a young age.

As a young girl, she was "Fast" because she had to learn the game quick.

As a woman, she's "Fast" because she's quick to play no games.

September 12, 2019 - Goldie

Men name cars.

I named you... Goldie.

Not only because of your color and how you reflect the sun, but because of your essence. Gold.

You are not just a vehicle. You are a vehicle of God. You are an answer to a very specific prayer. Like gold... You are a physical manifestation of an internal value. Gold once backed the US dollar. Thus your power, your essence. You can represent corn, cattle, or any human value at the marketplace. You are a universal form of currency.

More than a vehicle. You are a vehicle of God.

You empower me to save time. You are a time machine. You travel me from point A to point B with no complaints. You don't argue. If you are not feeling well, you show me a warning light. I respond. You don't expect me to read your mind. I appreciate that. Our communication is smooth. Our journey is the same... Smooth.

Thank you, Goldie.

September 30, 2019 - Thank You

Thank you for being a willing servant and beloved accomplice. Thank you for allowing Gods presence to flow through you. Thank you for anticipating my needs and responding with action. Do you know that you are an answered prayer? Do you understand that you carry God's Will in your heart.

I can't imagine how painful it was for you to become "you". I can't imagine having such power with no vision. Being vulnerable to men who exploited your value knowing that you were blind to it. Knowing they could define you because you lacked the power to define yourself. You've learned so many hard lessons on your path to me. Thank you for surviving. Thank you for evolving. Thank you for opening your eyes and seeing your light. Your love is seasoned with consciousness. You don't love me from an insecurity. You love me from the power of self-awareness. You know who you are, what you possess, and who to give it to.

That's why I smile through the hardest of times. For even if circumstances blind me from seeing my own superpower, I have you as a divine reminder...A divine reflection.

Thank you.

September 30, 2019 - Foreign Eyes

She looked at him in awe as she read his manuscript. Marking the page with her thumb, she looked off into space and whispered "Amazing..." as she rested the book in her lap.

He asked her to elaborate.

She said "You have a true gift. It's almost scary. You have the power to tell people what to do...and they do it." She continued..."If I had that gift, I'd have to be very careful not to abuse it. Literally, you say it and it gets done."

She questioned why he wasn't in a better position in life. She was amazed. As if he had access to a genie who grants wishes.

Why don't you ask for more?

He listened to her as if she wasn't talking to him. He didn't see himself the way she did. Perhaps it was his naturally tendency to be humble. Perhaps it was a hangover from a low-income mentality. Perhaps it was a lack of vision and self-awareness.

Either way, her perspective was foreign. She wasn't from America. She saw him thru unblemished eyes. The fact she saw him so clearly awakened something in his spirit. Even if he couldn't see what she saw, he felt the conviction of her vision. Which inspired him to be more of who he was...to speak more into existence. Thus, the spirituality of life and the power of energetic connections. Especially those with foreign eyes...

October 1, 2019 - Savor Me

The "like" I feel for you tastes like love. The like I feel for you smells like heaven. This is the type of like that is better than love. It's the feeling of something new. Something that can be potentially dangerous, potentially fun. You know that loving me would never work. Love would be too extreme. The beauty of this liking would be destroyed. This is meant for savoring. Once swallowed the experience dies.

October 2, 2019 - See Me See You

I want to know your presence in another way. I want to drink wine, naked, sitting on pillows. Candles and frankincense. I want to see candle light dancing in your eyes while you tell me your deepest truths. I want to see tears develop as you revisit the trauma and fight yourself for opening up too much... Sharing too much... Going too deep...

Being too vulnerable.

I want you to feel that realization in its totality.

Then I want to see your face transform as you realize that what you feel... with me... is Trust. That's a big deal for you. That's why I like you. That's why we are energetically possible.

We are each other. Oneness in action.

I want to witness your fear meet my trust.

I want you to feel seen. There is great magic in being fully perceived without judgment. Perception feels different when it comes from a righteous space.

I want you to see me see you.

October 3, 2019

I wish that I could share this view with you. I wish that you could "insperience" this experience with me. Tonight. No kids. No bills. No past. No future. Just the moment.

I wish that I could hold you from behind and just soak it in.

Just us. Me and you. Secluded on this mountain side. Overlooking everything. Simply because that's who we are. Overseers of everything.

You haven't seen me in a while. But we've mastered the art of distance love. It doesn't affect us. In fact, we needed it to grow into this awareness of who we are...to each other.

Your silent support bumps through the speakers of my soul. Your tough love tenderizes my heart. You stimulate my childhood ambition to "take care of my mom". I am possessed by a desire to please you. To make sure you're ok.

I'm tempted to wish that we had worked out...

You were created for me, but I wasn't ready for you. I had to find myself first. And you were assigned to assist me at your own expense. You were assigned to cultivate me and nurture me into my selfhood...then watch me fly away. But there is great beauty is in your watching. The spirituality of our bond is manifested in your vision. You gave yourself to me only to watch me fly away with what you gave me. But you kept watching. You kept holding on. And when your hands weren't strong enough to hold me, you held me with your gaze.

You watched me fly. Trusting that one day I'd do right
by your gift, your giving, and give back.
    I wish I could give you this view...
    I wish that I could share this with you.

October 7, 2019 - Celebrating Freedom/ Convict Conviction

Ten years ago, today, I won my freedom after being incarcerated for 18 years. I remember walking the yard and sharing my vision with brothers prior to release. Some of them could easily see my vision. Others thought that I was being unrealistic. I didn't mind because I understood that their lack of vision was simply an unhealthy download from The System. I understood that if the boldness of my vision could just serve as a 'seed of possibility', that would be enough. Everyone isn't built to have supernatural faith. Everyone isn't built to trust their gifts. I was a convict with conviction.

I came home and picked up my clippers just to make sure I was self-employed. I started my career at a day spa in the suburbs. (Changed my circle.) A gentleman who ran a hospital approached me about serving his staff. Clippers and conviction. I wanted my own shop and I wanted it to be more than a barbershop because I am more than a barber. I opened the first holistic spa inside a hospital. An administrative rep visited from California and told me I belonged on the west coast. She said I was in the wrong market. Midwest people weren't ready for my business. I came to California based on the conviction in her voice.

My partner has since expanded the business and I'm strolling the beach in San Diego celebrating my freedom anniversary. Alone. Me and the presence of God. I took a picture to capture the moment and I swore I saw a cross in the sky. But maybe I'm tripping. Maybe that's just me and my unrealistic vision. Convict Conviction

October 29, 2019 - B*tch

She had perfected the role of bitch. I didn't mind. I knew it was a role. She seemed to think that confrontation was a good thing. She'd push back on topics that didn't require it. Even casual conversations could lead to a debate with her. Every time she became forceful,

I'd fall back and just smile. I'd never meet her resistance with a response. I'd just smile at her. We ended up back at her place after cocktails. She seemed a bit loose but I couldn't tell if it was the alcohol or if she was just extra flirty. I had no interest in having sex and we had discussed it. She was adamant that inviting me to her home wasn't about sex. I agreed.

Our conversations were always great, but in the safety of her home they became even deeper. She cried a deep cry. Out of nowhere. We were discussing the past. She reached her childhood and a wave of emotion came over her. She sobbed from deep within her soul. She reached out to me for comfort. I held her and reassured her that it wasn't her fault. She had become a bitch to protect herself from her father. She was a leader to women, but to men...she was a natural bitch.

Her attitude radiated from a false concept of self. Being a bitch was the only way to feel comfortable at night when he would come into her room and fondle her while she slept. She had suffered too many of these nights as a lil girl. Finally she stood her ground and defended her body from him. It was hard to tell him no. He was her dad. She was supposed to love him, she was supposed to follow his lead, but she hated his guts. The day she rose up against him was pivotal. Rage pushed her to say "NOOOOO!" She felt mean. She felt guilty for being mean. She felt guilty for saying no. But enough was enough. She exploded. Her ability to repress her feelings didn't work anymore. In her rage she felt liberated...respected for the first time. In that moment "Bitch" became her salvation.

She carried that costume with her when she met me. I saw past it and she wondered how. After she emptied her reservoir of tears she asked me "Why did you stay? I've been so mean to you. Why didn't you run?"

I explained, there was nothing to run from. Her attitude had nothing to do with me. She was in conflict with a ghost from the past.

I saw her as a creation of God. She saw herself as the product of trauma. I provided a space for her spirit to transcend her conditioning.

That's all.

November 2. 2019 - Veteran (Vet Broad)

In the hood we'd call her a Vet Broad...

She was the older, more seasoned, version of Woman.

Grounded. Grown. On point.

She'd let you run the streets all day and you'd return to a 1st class meal, your game on the TV, beer in a frozen mug, and a tall glass of water with a lemon in it.

She wasn't needy. She had been married. She knew how to take care of a man. She was proud of the fact. Well-aware that she was worth coming home to, she never sweated the small stuff.

She loved on her own terms. The only thing missing from her life was a man to share certain moments with. Moments like now. Where she gets to obtain the deep joy of anticipating a man's needs.

She was a real woman. A true nurturer. Not once concerned with you taking anything from her.

She gave because she was a giver. It was her nature. And not many men were worthy of what she had to give, so when you found yourself in the grace of her presence, you could somehow sense why some women were considered queens. Her energy was different. Her love had a different texture. Like expensive bed sheets...she'd make you conscious of how good your body felt before escorting you to dreamland.

November 20, 2019 - Protect the Connect

I know how to suffer a consequence without saying a word. To catch a case without making a statement. I know how to take responsibility for an action. As a kid in the store with my mom, she would say "Don't touch it if you can't buy it!" That simple awareness taught me responsibility. I don't make moves that I can't afford to make. And I don't make thirsty moves. I can walk backwards and revisit any relationship I've ever had because I don't burn bridges. Through my character, my gifts, and my calling, I have travelled coast to coast trusting my ability to connect with the right people. It never fails.

The game of life is like the dope game. Your advancement depends on your grind and your "connect". Once you get the connect, you must protect the connect. That's an essential key to success. "The Connect" is anyone who expands your circle of influence, rather emotionally, financially, or spiritually. All relationships are connections. And I am proud to say...

I protect the connect.

November 21, 2019 - The Female Ego

The female ego is a mysterious creature. She speaks in code and communicates by insinuation. Men's actions become perceived through that lens. The lens of insinuation. She's always on alert for things that don't line up. Inconsistencies. Red flags. So much so that she can find them any and everywhere. Love is legal. She operates from the disposition of a prosecutor. She loves you and builds a case against you at the same time.

It's not necessarily her fault. She was conditioned to distrust the human soul. She feels alone and misunderstood. Everyone has crossed her.

What she doesn't understand is that she has a part to play in it. This is where spirituality would aid her.
Secular people question human motives. They're prepared to defend themselves.

Spiritual people trust God as the source and provider of their needs. They expect blessings. They also see God in themselves. Ultimately, accepting their roles in the creation of their realities.

The reality of the female ego is dark, lonely, sometimes messy, always unsure. Which drives it to be right. Once it suspects something it will move to confirm it. She doesn't understand that this is the source of her dis-ease. The lack of trust in herself produces lack of trust in others. She'll ask you a question, already knowing the answer, just to see how you respond.

She's sharp and calculated. Strong and afraid. Tender and vulnerable...

And I can't help but love her.

December 4, 2019 - White Chocolate

No one talks about how she's a revolutionary... How she single-handedly destroyed racism in her own household. No one celebrated the moment she brought a black man home and secretly dared her dad not to accept him. Her father was a closet racist. All of that died when the biracial baby was born...The extra beautiful child who became the star of all the grandchildren. The special child.

No one applauded her victory.

She was the black sheep of her family and black women looked at her as a thief...as if she had stolen a black man. She couldn't win. Yet she persevered and overcame.

Her family relaxed their old school conditionings. Evolved sistas embraced her as extended family. She prevailed in breaking down barriers and challenging stereotypes.

But no one talks about how she's a revolutionary.

I will...

Thank you,
White Chocolate.

December 14, 2019 - Uncarcerated Sun

He witnessed Ultimate Freedom thru prison bars. Freedom had taken him from the Midwest to the west coast. Bigger, better, broader. But at the edge of freedom was the ocean... Ultimate Freedom. A mating ritual performed by the sun and the sea.

To join the movement of procreation he had to challenge the bars of limitation. He needed to liberate himself from the familiar.

He had travelled thus far on safely paved roads, sophisticated highways, and planes. To experience Ultimate Freedom he had to not only swim, he had to swim amongst sharks. The idea of being in unfamiliar terrain with unknown predators was terrifying.

He didn't know that right beyond his self-imposed prison was Christ in the form of a speed boat. It was already worked out. He just needed a mustard seed of faith.

He was trying to figure out something that only required his trust.

January 23, 2020 - Praying Upside Down

She prayed upside down as if praising the devil,
All the while, exercising her oneness with God
On whole different level.
Spiritual seduction.
Her image...an example of what happens when you make love to discipline.
She French kisses stillness,
Quiets the mind
Assumes the complicated pose
Of the moment she totally owns.
She breathes slowly through her nose,
Exhaling everything that needs to go.
She prayed upside down.

January 24, 2020 - Reminder to Self

There's a moment when the opponent (circumstance) presents itself and the first ponds are pushed. The mind weighs the character of the situation and pairs it with the best strategy. It reaches into the future and sets up the board accordingly. Each move comes with multiple variables. Situating the variables in your favor becomes the goal. That's the game.

A chess player can't afford to be one dimensional. He can't afford to be narrow minded or trapped in old thinking patterns. Adapting to personalities (situations) is the name of the game.

My mentor would position the board in such a way that my next move would be critical. Understanding the gravity of the moment he'd quietly say...

"Make your next move your best move."

Reminder to self...

February 12, 2020 - The Christian Witch

She was a Christian Witch. Her eyes were a blend of darkness and light. The hazel behind her pupils appeared to be an eclipse... The moon appearing black as it covered the sun. She was a paradox. God fearing and dangerous.

Her body carried a spirit that exceeded her physical presence. She radiated an energy that inspired curiosity. In the "infamous" interview Mr. Trump said that when he saw beautiful women he had to kiss them. "I can't help myself."

She was the type of woman to stimulate this urge in men. Which is why historically she'd be burned at the stake. She made men lose control. Better to demonize her and destroy her than to deal with the power she embodies.

Born into her power she didn't understand it as a little girl. Men were drawn to her and she didn't understand why. This led to abuse. She became sexualized and burdened with guilt. As she grew older, she learned to harness her power. She played with it as a teenager. She mastered it as a young woman. She cloaked herself in Christianity to guard herself from social judgment. She attempted to blend in but she couldn't help but stand out. Wives shunned her and made sure their husbands stayed away from her. She understood female insecurity, that's why she stayed in her lane. Always polished and professional. Always poised. Non-threatening. Yet women still feared her. Hated her for no reason.

She was unmoved by their hostility. Comfortable in her own skin because she understood a spirit lives there. A spirit that was connected to the universe, the Source.

Nature was her companion. Sunshine, Rain, Oceans, were her friends. She didn't need people. She was turned on by the Creator, which is why she was so powerful.

February 14, 2020 - The Side Nigga

Dear Bra,

I encourage you to take a different approach with your woman. Accusing me of being her "side nigga" isn't going to help your cause. Accusing her of cheating with me isn't going to advance your position with her. I was here before you. I will be here after you. I know she loves you. I know the past flames that she randomly still talks to. You have every right to think that I'm more than a friend, because I am.

Outside of being her friend, I'm an advocate for you!

There have been countless times where you have fucked up and she has called me. Countless times when I have talked her into forgiving you because I know how much she loves you. I know that you aren't the right man for her but I'd never say that. I'd never demonize a man she loves. Instead, I encourage her to love you more.

Why? Because I'm a real friend and I understand her love language.

She's been attracting dysfunction for years. Each dysfunctional relationship builds her character. She has the tendency to learn things the hard way.

I know you don't really want her as your woman. You only seek to keep her under your spell and away from other men. I get it Bra. But I'd never expose what you're doing because she's smart enough to figure it out. I support her in what she thinks is right. If I speak against you, I speak against a man she loves. My word would lose credibility. She would hear me, but she wouldn't listen. I'd be perceived as a hater. And this is what you're doing by speaking against my name.

Please stop trying use me as a weapon. You're only shortening your life span with her. And when it ends...I'll still remain.

Sincerely,
The Side Nigga

February 18, 2020 - Felonious Love

A man who has served time in prison is a man who has learned how to live without women. He's a challenge to love because of this fact. Losing your freedom and lifestyle will change you. It will make you resourceful in ways you can't imagine. You learn how to take repressed sexual energy and channel it into different areas of your life, your hustle, your grind.

To love him is to subject yourself to a person who can lose you and live without you. After all, he lost everything in the past and rebuilt from nothing. He knows how to survive. This reality will haunt the relationship. At times it may cause you to question your value to him. It may cause you to question your self-worth. Am I enough?

In his life, everything comes and goes. He doesn't take things personally. Incarceration creates a core need for freedom. You can only love him with freedom. There can be no captivity.

You'll have to understand that his primary value is freedom. He protects his freedom and his space. Make yourself a part of his freedom and you make yourself a part of his space. It's a simple equation but only an evolved woman can do it.

March 4, 2020 - Voicing Her Needs

"Are you the type of woman to secretly expect him to understand your needs? Or are you the type to make your needs known?"

Her explanation told me a lot. Somehow, she equated voicing her needs with begging. On a deeper level, since she lacked the ability to voice her needs she found magic in a man's ability to figure them out. "If a man really cares, he'll look for answers. He'll figure it out."

I chose not to criticize her strategy, instead, I asked her how important time was. She had wasted lots of time in relationships that didn't work out because her needs were never met. She shows up as "the giver" in an unconscious effort to show men how she wants to be loved. But men don't get the message. They grow comfortable in the comfort she intentionally provides. She would grow to criticize them for being users. All of the men in her past followed the same pattern.

Now she doesn't love so openly. She hesitates to give herself out of fear of not being appreciated which translates into not being enough. She didn't know where she was going wrong. She knew that she was a good woman she just didn't understand how to transform that into a healthy relationship. She asked me if she was wrong?

"I don't care about right or wrong. I care about math and you are the common denominator of your experiences. You don't show up for relationships because you want to be found. That's what I hear you saying...that's what I see you creating. Once someone finds you, they lose you. Too you, love is a treasure hunt. Once the treasure is found the hunt is over. If you want to change the practice, you have to change the theory."

March 20, 2020 - The Hole

In prison there is a place called "The Hole". It's where they send you for punishment. 23-hour lockdown and you're fed through a slot in the door like an animal. Our situation will get much tighter but you will never experience this level of isolation.

My mother got highly concerned during the time I went there. She didn't understand my peace. She thought I was trying to be strong to protect her feelings. But I wasn't. I was truly at peace. When you are stripped of all external distractions TV, radio, etc. you go within. I was fighting for freedom and being in the hole couldn't stop my efforts to achieve my goal. Going within was the most beautiful thing that ever happened to me. It tapped me into a power that I wasn't using while I had distractions.

In such a time you learn what true power is. Isolation was the birthplace of my spirituality.

Now that movement has stopped. We are realizing how precious freedom is. Our values are being realigned. A shift is taking place. There will be a huge rebound from this experience. Use this time to visualize where you want to be on the other end of it. Use this time to intentionally connect with people who are doing what you want to be doing. Network with people who are passionate about creation.

Everyone is reminded of their mortality. Use this time to heal from the past. Reach out to someone who hurt you and forgive them verbally. Apologize to someone you've done wrong. Do something freaky with your lover.

Resist the urge to be afraid and exercise your power of intimacy and healing.

-Spoken Sol

March 21, 2020

I witness you as you witness the stillness of life...

I have your back.

As you suffer the beauty of isolation...

As the home you built for security becomes a source of captivity. A beautiful prison.

I have your back.

As you gaze out the window, thinking about all the responsibilities you no longer have...

As you wonder "What's next?"...

Seduced by the illusion of the future, and all the uncertainties within it...

As you play out possibilities that you have no control over.

As you stir up anxiety, losing sight of the now...

I have your back.

I witness you as you witness the stillness of life...

You are not alone. I have your back. And if you could see what I see, you'd see organic beauty.

Captured in a moment.

March 23, 2020 - Domestic Violence

What do I look like arguing with you over your perception of yourself?

I say you're thick. You say you're fat. Ok.

On to the next.

You know yourself better than I do. Who am I to argue with you?

I love you as you are. But you seek to be other than yourself.

By all accounts you are worth keeping, loving, and protecting, but somehow you don't really know it.

I'm not judging.

I'm just choosing not to argue.

I once loved a woman with body dysmorphia. She lost lots of weight but she looked in the mirror and still saw a fat girl. I couldn't comprehend it. As a result, it redefined our relationship. I began to look at her the way she looked at herself... and that shit wasn't cool. It was painful.

And I'm not turned on by domestic violence.

March 23, 2020 - Sincerely Sport Coat

When you disregard her, you make her feel unworthy.

When you overlook her, you make her feel invisible.

She calls me when she needs to be seen.

I see her... The beautiful mess that she is.

I see her without judgment. She loves that. In turn, she loves me even more.

Sometimes she looks at me and I can see her trying to visualize you. She tries to imagine herself having fun with you like she has with me. Organic fun. Simple, engaged, connected, conversation. That's all she wants. She doesn't need gifts or things. She craves intimacy. The way you treat her only stimulates that need.

When your love confuses her...

When you create an issue that causes her frustration...

When you make her think she's trippin...

You destabilize her. She seeks grounding through my presence.

You do just enough to keep her but you make it very easy for her to stray.

A lesser man would take advantage of her vulnerability. He'd grant her the satisfaction of kissing you with the sweet taste of revenge on her tongue...

But I live by a particular constitution. Not all men live by my code.

Tighten up my friend.

Sincerely,
Sport Coat

March 24, 2020

There was great beauty in his dysfunction. He had the ability to be present but unattached. It's a skill he learned in prison. To be in it, but not of it. This "present detachment" extended into his personal relationships. This made him complicated to love.

She cried to him in anguish "You can't live life disregarding people's feelings the way you do!" But he wasn't the kind of man to live life according to anyone's feelings. He was convinced that he had a calling. God was his guide. He didn't wake up every morning thinking about being a husband. He woke up thinking about being a builder, a servant. His spirituality hindered his ability to love on secular terms.

She wanted him to tend her emotions and reassure her that everything would be ok. In his mind, everything was ok...even if it wasn't. His reassurance came from God. Not people. So it was difficult for him to express compassion in a way that she'd understand. He gave the impression that he didn't care. In truth, his ability to care was directed to God.

She needed to know that he loved her different from anyone else, so she asked him directly "Do you love me, or are you "in love" with me...? And don't give me that spiritual shit!!"

He smiled and responded, "I am love."

"Fuck you!"

"When?"

Lol.

March 24, 2020

She was one with earth...

So much so, that she became a legend in the imaginations of skeptics. Oral historians of hidden villages had spoken about her. The woman who was "One with All". They described her as a shape shifter. She could become anything because she was everything. Skeptics had debated her existence for years. Those who knew she existed would say "Where do you think the idea of mermaids came from?"

Both sides had their points.

One day, there was a starving artist roaming the woods. She was hungry for evidence of God. Her relationship with her camera was spiritual. As prayer is communicating with God, her camera would capture evidence of God. Being in nature made her feel connected. Conscious of the small blessings that become miracles. And there it was...

A space that was worthy of capturing. An opening... A stream that was colored green from reflecting the trees, highlighted by light grey stones.

It was beautiful.

It was a moment.

Then the miracle occurred. The forefront of the picture became the background as the mythical creature suddenly arose for air.

There and gone yet captured in the moment.

Moral: Seek oneness with God and God will exceed your expectations.

March 26, 2020 - Nakeda

She is a Black Woman... A Natural Sista.

In the Mother country the village called her MaMa.

She's a matriarch. We went to her for counsel.

On matters of war, love, and culture. Her word was Law.

She taught us how to plant by the moon, chart the stars, And sing salutations to the sun.

Her voice was a trumpet, a call to action.

She taught us accountability, purpose of being, knowledge of self.

Her intuition was the whisper of God, guiding us inward.

She taught us our bodies are temples, vehicles, and instruments of healing.

She taught us the power of stillness and the art of listening.

I thank God for her as I thank her for her.

She is a Black Woman... A Natural Sista.

March 27, 2020 - He Said She Said

She said- You're selfish

He said- I know.

She said- You say that like you're proud of it.

He said- I'm agreeing with you.

She said- But you act like it's a good thing.

He said- You act like it's a bad thing.

She said- It is!!! We're supposed to be selfless.

He said- That doesn't make sense. You can't give what you don't have.

You must have self to give self. If you are self "less" what is there to give? And this is why she never talked to him about her feelings.

He was impossible.

March 30, 2020

Submit to Me your discipline and, in return, I'll give you grace beyond your imagination. I'll form you into a star. Have you ever seen a celebrity enter a room? Do you know why we call them stars?

I'll make you the center of attention because all your attention is given, solely, to Me. You see Me everywhere. So everywhere you are, people will see Me. They will witness a person who somehow resembles Me. A person looking for Me, being Me. It will be undeniable.

From the Sun, comes a Star.

You are.

March 31, 2020

Darkness erases vision. But there was no amount of darkness that could make her invisible. She was created to shine. Even in the darkest of times her spirit would illuminate her being. The fire in her belly would rise to her breasts, in the form of wings. Giving flight to her heart. Elevating her mind. Effortlessly escaping the cage of darkness.

Her lips were neon weapons. Instruments of song. She would sing thru a hard time. Dance thru a dark time. People thought she was crazy. She was just "ok" with being alone. She'd throw a 30-minute pity party that would become all night jam session.

Even when she took a loss, she reaped a gain.

Darkness came...

She remained.

April 1, 2020 - Holding On

A woman who lacks self-knowledge will seek her definition through the presence of a man.

Her "liking" him will become "loving" him in a very short period of time. She will unconsciously rush the relationship into fruition because she needs to be needed. It won't happen naturally. The man who grows to like her will go along with the process. Her thirst for attention will stroke his ego.

He will find reasons to create distance from her. She will fight to erase the distance. Any time he is away from her she will suspect him of being with another woman. She will be correct. Her insecurities will manifest the symptoms of stalking. She will monitor him. She will keep track of him. Ultimately, she will find that he's been seeing other women. It's inevitable.

They will fall out. The falling out will only prepare the atmosphere for great "make up sex".

There, he will satisfy her need to have him to herself. From that point on, it will be the only time she feels secure.

When he is away the ghosts will reappear and she'll begin to imagine who else he's spending time with. She will text him while he's at work. Counting the minutes until he responds. His attention will become an obsession, a drug. She will appear clingy but she's just holding on.

April 4, 2020

She was cut from a different cloth. The descendant of an ancient culture of Wild Women who understood darkness and bathed in the sun. Female warrior types. Women who understood power and how to command it.

In society, she had to manage her power. Distribute it in doses. Package it. Refine it.

In nature, she was free of 'all things human'. Free to be a spirit flowing through a body. Dancing in the wind. Naked and unashamed.

Pale winter skin encouraging Spring. Celebrating sun rays, holding nothing back.

Absent of the need to divide self with tan lines.

Darkness brought her joy

April 9, 2020 - Quarantined Marriage

I chimed in with one of my clients today. He comes for a buzz cut but really he just pays me to vent and receive advice. He hates his wife.

He loves her for the mother she is but he hates her as a wife. They ignore each other. They don't care to talk. She's not interested in him. He's not interested in her. He provides. She manages. It's an arrangement.

He resents her because he doesn't feel appreciated for what he provides.

Now he's stuck with her. They are cell mates. Work was usually his escape. Now he's working from home. He feels trapped. He asked me what he should do. I know their story intimately.

I told him that resentment, anger, rage, were all forms of passion. I asked him if he could manipulate those energies to his benefit. He was confused.

He had become passive. He had lost his vigor as a man. He thought that "providing" was the extent to his manhood. He felt like his job was done. He wasn't giving her energy.

I used breakfast as a teaching tool to illustrate my point. He had grown to eat whatever she cooked. I encouraged him to make a request. Be specific about your eggs and be particular about bacon. She was used to frying it. I told him to have her bake it.

His instant response was he didn't want to bother her with small stuff. As long as the kids were fine, he was fine. He didn't want to burden her. Not understanding that what he perceived as a burden was actually interaction. She needed him to need her. She wanted him to get involved and express his desires.

He acted as if he didn't care...and that lack of concern extended to her libido. There was nothing between them. No spark. No engagement. They had nothing but the appearance of a happy family. Quarantine revealed a truth they had been ignoring for so long.

Wedding season is here. Sadly, so is divorce.

April 9, 2020 - Dear Moon

You control the tide. The tide effects emotions.
I have ridden your highest waves, in the body of foreign oceans.

She waved at me. Of all the waves that poured from the horizon

She clearly stood out as the one.

I eyed her and followed her motions, positioning my surfboard to approach her. The closer she came, the higher she rose. When waves exceed normal capacity, training becomes invalid.

I relied on my instincts. Male intuition. I was here for this moment. This opportunity. My training took me as far as I could go. I mounted her. She rapidly began to rise. Three times normal size. Lost sight of my balance because I couldn't believe my eyes. Never made it to her tunnel. I took a dive. No surprise.

No tears to cry, there's pride in the try.

Waves are abundant hellos.

Tides rise to say goodbye.

April 16, 2020 - Facebook Queen

She was a Facebook queen. Like most men play video games, she played social media.

Her inbox was scandalous. A source of frustration and entertainment. Men lined up for her attention. On a good day the attention was flattering. On a bad day it was disgusting. Married men approaching her. Guys with girlfriends. No one was loyal. It made her lose faith in men. Which made her lose faith in herself. "Why am I not enough?".

She was enough to cheat with, but not enough to commit to. And every commitment she ever had resulted in cheating. She wasn't innocent. She had cheated as well.

I suggested that she entertain the idea of an open relationship. She shunned me.

"That's not what I want. That's not who I am."

I gently pointed out that she had never been in a relationship that didn't involve cheating.

Thus, all of her relationships, in fact, had been, open.

Summary: If you consciously shun something that you unconsciously practice, you are shunning yourself. My wish for her was true love. No shame, guilt, or distrust. Open relationships offer that. Love based on choice, not emotional obligation. It was just a suggestion...

April 17, 2020 - Spiritual D Pic

I was speaking to my spiritual friend about dating and today's culture. She expressed how she enjoyed one of my posts. It was personal and showed her a glimpse of who I was in a private way. I laughed and called the post a "spiritual dick pic". We had a good laugh. But the idea stayed with me.

In a culture of push button love and immediate gratification, the infamous dick pic is a man's way of showing what he's working with. An intimate post about love is the same thing. It's a portrait of man's capacity to love. It's an image of "what he's working with". Rather than sexual, it's spiritual. It's expresses a man's ability to feel deeply, arouse interest, stimulate thought...which is connection on a deeper level.

Inner course.

Intercourse.

Of course.

April 17, 2020 - Meditation

In prison I learned a meditation technique. To escape from the chaos of the environment I'd travel inside of my heart. I'd visualize the woman of my dreams and I'd allow my heart to flow to her. I'd zone out seeking to connect with her spirit, hoping to attract her into my reality.

She reminded me of you. Beautiful in a holistic way. Natural, healthy, spiritually aware. Her heart was tenderized by pain. She understood loss. She understood victory. Small victories. She was a virago.

I promised her that when I came home, I'd shower her with the deepest of intimacies. She had been with men who had money. She had built men up and saw them betray the love she had given. She was seasoned enough in affairs of love to know exactly what she needed to feel emotional bliss. She wasn't looking for anything mediocre. In fact, she wasn't looking for anything. She intuitively understood that if it existed, it would show up. The love she wanted was the love she cultivated within herself. She was clothed in her own love. God's love.

As spiritual as she was, she was still a woman. A passionate woman. Ripe with affection. What she wanted most from a man was presence and time. Conscious, intentional, time.

I was the perfect man for her. A conscious man can only love a conscious woman (in a romantic way). The gifts God gave me were meant for her.

She reminds me of you.

April 18, 2020 - Like vs Love

There is no guarantee that you will always like me on this journey. Like is your choice. Love is a choice that was made for you. So, when you find yourself upset with me, I will give you space to be upset. My responsibility is to remain in a state of love.

It will seem like I don't care about your feelings. It will seem heartless. But really, I'm just honoring myself by staying true to the guarantee. The guarantee of love. In honoring myself, I hope to honor you by allowing you time to process your feelings. After all, they belong to you. You choose them. They are your responsibility.

You will eventually come around. You will eventually get past the anger and return to love. And there I will stand waiting, loving, being.

April 18, 2020 - Accusation

"We use defense in the presence of offense. Thus, if you defend yourself that means you're being offended."
- Amen-Ra

She asked me to defend myself. I refused. I wasn't offended. The question, alone, was a statement that ended our relationship. If a woman questions her trust for a man, trust is gone. And where there is no trust, there is no love. It's a simple equation of human relations. So rather than argue a case I couldn't win, I accepted the truth of the matter. She didn't trust me, which means she couldn't use me, and if she couldn't use me, I held no value. That's business.

The tragedy is, I came to her seeking to be used at a time when she needed exactly who I was. We met and our relationship happened. It had its own definition based on our immediate, individual, needs. Right place, right time. Destiny. Answered prayer. All of that.

You can end the relationship but how do you end the spiritual connection?

There is no such thing.

When you have a spirit of discernment and trust of God, you don't have an appetite for manufactured relationships. When you trust God relationships are organic. If they cease to be organic, they cease to be. There is no offense...there is just truth. Which needs no defending.

April 20, 2020 - Almost Love

She didn't really want to love. She wanted to play. She wanted to pretend that she was beyond getting hurt. She wanted to play the relationship game...
"Get you before you get me".

It was extremely hard to get past her divorce. Once she did, that part of her was locked away. Forbidden from men.

She loved men on her own terms. Those terms were a product of her divorce and she wasn't even conscious of it.

She thought that she was over the pain of her divorce. But she had only learned how to live with the pain. Like a person who suffers from chronic back pain. You still must work, you still have to move on. She moved on.

She was still capable of love. Just not the love that would sweep you away. That real love! She had to control the current.

Her husband taught her how to love. He abused her with financial stability. Now she was an abuser disguised as a lover. She would spoil you into captivity. The same thing her husband did to her.

She didn't really want to love. She wanted to love on her own terms. And, in love, there is no such thing.

April 20, 2020 - Belonging

She clung to him as if he was life. Breathing him deeply.

She'd bask in his light as if he was the sun. He was the very source of her vitamin D.

She needed him to feel well. As a rainy day stimulates depression, his radiance was something of an existential aphrodisiac. It not only made her feel alive, it turned her on.

She was crazy about him. Nothing about their relationship made sense. It wasn't intellectual. It was a feeling. A spiritual suspicion. An impulse.

She felt born to serve him.

She had given herself to many men. She had given her heart, her mind, her body, and her capabilities. She had sacrificed her needs to make it work. She understood the defeat. Her failed marriage was a symbol of this reality. Yet, something about him inspired her to serve. She couldn't help it. Even when her mind tried to hold her back her spirit persisted, sensing the danger of deliverance.

He opened her up and let her go. Like a sunray to the fragrance of an obedient rose. He was incapable of taking her personal. Yet, she needed to be taken, claimed, owned.

She was the rose in nature that wanted to be taken home and placed in a vase. In his mind, such an action would deprive her of the life she was meant to live.

They spoke two different languages.

He didn't understand that she belonged to him.

She didn't understand that he belonged to God.

April 21, 2020 - Kissing a Republican

She was white. He was black. She was suburban, he was from the city, yet they had many things in common.

She was skeptical about meeting him at first. During their early conversations she was quick to find reasons why they wouldn't get along. He was far too liberal. She was conservative. He was an artist. She was an organizer. But she loved his eyes, his conversation, and his style. He was different. She agreed to meet. No harm in that.

There was instant chemistry. His eyes were more powerful in person. She was used to intimidating men but he wasn't. He held her stare. In fact, he seemed to look through her. The meeting went well. He walked her to her car and hugged her goodbye. As he walked away, she extended the conversation. Small talk. Just something to keep him present. She wasn't ready for him to leave but she didn't want to appear thirsty or desperate. He understood. He turned towards her and approached. Looking in her eyes, he closed the distance without saying a word. He planted his lips on her cheek and held her one last time. She embraced him with more conviction. Rubbing his broad shoulders as his unique scent flooded her senses. His lips found hers and she welcomed him. The fullness of his oral presence overwhelmed her. His lips were soft and deliberate. He kissed her with his teeth, nibbling her lips firmly. He massaged them with his tongue to remove the discomfort. His tongue explored the landscape of her mouth, tracing her lips, riding her gum line, and diving into her throat. It was a nasty, intentionally messy, kiss. He sucked her tongue dry before cleaning up the mess he had made. She gasped and held him closer, grinding her torso into his erection. She wanted to fuck. It was obvious.

He concluded the kiss the way it began. With a soft peck on her cheek.

She watched him as he walked away, too turned on to call him back. It was supposed to be a casual meet and greet but it turned into foreplay as her imagination went wild with possibilities...

After all, she was conservative. This wasn't supposed to be happening. She had rules and protocols for this type of thing. But none of that mattered. He inspired her to be free. To break the rules. She wanted more... Right now.

But he was gone...

Fuckin liberals!

April 23, 2020 - Social Media Crush

My social media crush posted a picture of her hand with an engagement ring. Two emotions hit me. Joy and concern. Spiritually, I applauded her success and shook my head at the same time. Something didn't seem right about it. Shortly thereafter she posted that the engagement was off. She caught him cheating. This all happened in the same day.

I shook my head.

She was my type of woman. Her personality and values were clearly expressed thru the things she would post. Not only was she very attractive, but she was also grounded. The type of woman you wanted to come home to. The type to spoil her man. She knew that she was a rare catch and her love expressed that sentiment. She knew HOW to love. She was an emotional overachiever. Making you feel special was her superpower. It was her insurance over other women.

Her blessing was her curse. Since she was special, you'd have to prove yourself worthy of what she had to offer. You'd have to work to get past her guard. The problem is, in this culture, such a strategy lays the foundation for game. Courtship becomes conquest. Thus, after you acquire her, she instantly loses value because "love" gets lost in the game of acquisition.

April 24, 2020 - Conscious Love

There is nothing more sexy than conscious love. When you truly see the lover and accept them for who they are.

When who they are is something worth investing in, giving yourself to. Conscious love always gives a return on the investment. There is never a loss taken. You receive from giving. It's immediate. It doesn't require time. Which is why "love at first sight" is a real term. When you vibrate at a certain frequency, you'll recognize that frequency when it appears. There is no mistaking it. Conscious love isn't random, it's intentional.

Conscious lovers arrive with a sexualized presence. Self-love exudes from their being. When self-love sees itself reflected, amplification is the automatic result. You can't help but want to come together. Literally. Figuratively.

Another aspect of conscious love is boldness. The lovers don't fear taking a loss because their abundance is tied to God, not the object of affection.

May 11, 2020 - I am Love

I am a lover because I am love.

Love feels good. I choose love in all that I do. I'd rather write a love letter than debate politics. I'd rather be the vehicle for a poem than to argue with my beloved.

With love comes understanding. With understanding comes peace. With peace comes the highest possibility for pleasure.

Words are precious. Why argue?

Prison taught me how to use words to inspire orgasms.

I can tell you a story about yourself that will make you moist. You exist. You are already there. "Coming" means I allow you the space to be your true self.

I am a lover because I am love.

May 12, 2020 - Smiling Mugshot

She was happily arrested by the possibility of love. Her mugshot was a perfect selfie. She was captivating. Held captive by an image of herself that she would never live up to. Her digital self was a thirst trap for good guys. The kinda guys she liked...but didn't like. They were kinda soft. She was drawn to bad guys. Guys with edge. She needed you to be smart, articulate, and thuggish. It was a challenge for her to find the right blend.

Then there was him...

A bit of a paradox. He was transparent and it was very refreshing.

No guess work. No fine print. But he was also secretive. Very selective in his words. Not prone to discuss details. He was a product of the streets and discretion was his way of protecting loved ones. You can't be an informant if you don't have information. The less you knew the better. Rather on the golf course, in the hood, or a relationship, his perspective never changed. He'd protect you with discretion.

This turned her on. If gave her something to figure out. A challenge.

She was determined to break into his mind. She was caught...up.

The authorities cuffed her, booked her, and in her mugshot she smiled.

Happily arrested by the possibility of love.

May 12, 2020 - Mother Goddess

You are poetry in motion. A song of meditation. The voice of a bedtime story. You make me want to lay down... With you. Without you. Within you.

You make me want to breast feed. Instinctively suck nipples for survival. Within you is everything I need for life. Does that make you God? After all, before I could consciously pray I would instinctively cry, and you would rush to tend my needs.

In a single motion you would check the clock, calculate if I was hungry, sleepy, or messy. You'd check my Pamper, simultaneously, preparing my bottle or your breast.

Sounds like something God could do.

At least.. The Goddess in you.

May 15/2020 - I vs We

She was risking her individuality by entertaining him. He was dangerous. For some reason she couldn't walk away or talk herself out of his vibration. It was fucked up. She was losing her "I" to a WE that she didn't ask for. A WE she had no control over. Or maybe she did. Perhaps she was seducing him. Silly boy... lost in his spirituality and eastern philosophies. No match for a woman of her IQ. Or so she thought.

She was drawn to his mind. She saw herself in his convictions and she fell in love automatically. She had longed for a man of conviction. A man to challenge her. A psychological sparring partner. Her mind was an erogenous zone.

The more she entertained him the more she disappeared. It was magical. Surreal. She met him and something in her shifted. She studied his ways and looked for inconsistencies in his character. She needed to find a valid reason to walk away.

There were none. And this drove her crazy. She had grown to think that all men were the same. She was sure of it. So she pushed him and prodded. Searching for a reaction to justify her intuition. But she realized it wasn't her intuition speaking. It was her conditioning. He survived her assault, her rebellion, her protest. He somehow understood that she was really fighting herself and using him as a projection. The more she fought, the more she lost.

Losing was against her character, so she gave up. She was forced to yield to his spiritual loftiness and experience the beauty of winning by losing

May 16, 2020 - The Sweetest Goodbye

She gave the sweetest goodbyes. She broke up with him in the sweetest of ways. With those goodbyes came his absence, and with his absence came hunger. The silence between the goodbyes and the hellos was sometimes unbearable.

In those moments her empathy would take over. She would consider his needs. As always. And she knew that he needed her. She designed it that way. Her heart would move her to reach out to him, yet again, for the sake of quenching his thirst for her presence. But really, she was satisfying her hunger for his.

She gave the sweetest goodbyes...

May 20, 2020 - Worthy

Find a man who is worthy of your education. That's the challenge. When something comes natural to you it can be frustrating to teach it. It's a feeling. You just do it. You love. You express love by showing interest and making time. You call. You plan weekends. You show up. Be present. It's simple. Right? It can seem juvenile to have to explain it. Beneath you. In your mind, he should just know. It's not complicated.

Find a man who is worth of teachable moments. Mentally roll your eyes, take a deep yoga breath, exhale, and say "Fuck it! I'm going to have to show him."

Find a man worthy of that frustration and transform it into a beautiful opportunity for connection and growth. Have fun with love. Quit being so serious. So what "He's the man" and it should be natural for him to take the lead. If he doesn't love in your language, how can you hold him responsible for a conversation he can't possibly have.

The question is- why do you find it so offensive to teach what you are?

Your story taught you what true love is. His story may be different. He may not have a reference for the love you so intimately understand. Teaching him is reaching him.

I hope you find a man worth reaching. I hope you find a man who is worthy of your education.

May 21, 2020 - Natural Beauty

I paid a compliment to a beautiful woman only to find out she was ugly. She was dressed for errands. Athletic gear, ponytail, no make-up. Her skin was vibrant. Her eyes were captivating. I smiled "Good afternoon" and she smiled back and returned my greeting.

I told her that I thought she was a beautiful woman (and so she wouldn't think I was coming on to her) I added how much I love when my wife dresses like that. I'm a fan of natural beauty. She looked at me like I was crazy. I wished her a good day and kept moving.

Later I found out we were Facebook friends and I saw a post about "thirsty men". How they will compliment you even when you look gross at the grocery store.

I read the comments in total fascination. It seems that women resonate with this idea.
I'm not totally oblivious. I know some women who don't leave their house without make up.

I know women who won't post a picture without a filter. I get it.

But ladies, I promise you there is nothing more beautiful than a natural woman. And if a gentleman pays you a compliment, quiet your ego, and just receive it. Perhaps the universe is using a random stranger to tell you that you are enough, as you are, without the drag.

Damn.

May 22, 2020 - Trending

I've noticed an interesting trend since I've been actively playing with social media for the past 5 years. If an attractive woman posts something enlightened and spiritual there's not much response. But if she posts something provocative there's all sorts of comments. By provocative, it could be an edgy post about relationships, or a sexy picture. Either way there's interaction. But the intelligent posts get crickets.

I find that strange.

I wonder what it does to a woman's self-esteem to be unconsciously sexualized.

I'm using social media to find my audience. I understand the value of likes and shares. But if I was just using this for entertainment and the only way to be entertained was to be sexual... Hmmm... That's kinda fucked up.

May 30, 2020 - Spooning

Spoon with her and use the nape of her neck as a microphone. Whisper loudly. Her mind is a highway. Say something that will stop traffic. Validate her. Give her a reason to reflect on herself in a positive light. Give her a different kind of orgasm. An awakening.

Celebrate her silence. View her as a perfectly designed gift.

Intuit her trauma. Realize that everything she's been through made her perfect for you. Pull her into your erection and wrap your hand around her breast. Grip her.

Connect with her heartbeat. Maximize closeness. Breath with her.

Don't make love. Simply be the presence of love. Wrap her in it.

Show her the difference between an experience and an in-sperience.

June 8, 2020 - Bitter Sweet

I vow to treat you as an extension of myself... That sounds sweet, but it's a bitter reality. Why? Because I tend to forget myself sometimes.

I go on spurts where I become more focused on giving and helping. I lose myself to the people I love. Also within myself I have gifts and ideas. Sometimes I have so many ideas that I get lost in all of my options. Sometimes I lose myself in my ideas as I do with people I love.

What does this look like in a relationship?

It looks like me losing you at times. It looks like your needs being overlooked, sometimes, because my attention goes elsewhere. I do this with myself. If you are an extension of me, I will do it to you. But I vow to treat you as an extension of myself.

June 11, 2020 - Falling in Love

I fall in love too easy because I am love. It's easy to be myself. My being is designed to seek and serve. It's not something I can turn off. Where most men are programmed to mate, I'm programmed to procreate.

I'm not motivated by sex. I don't want your pussy. I want your trauma, your guilt, your void. I want the part of you that you only share with your best friend after drinking a bottle of wine. The part of you that you share with your therapist...or don't share at all.

A healer is most alive in the process of healing.

A light shines brightest in a background of darkness.

I want to be most alive with you. Feeding you light with the intention of healing. Taking care of you is taking care of myself, much like taking care of the earth is taking care of God.

June 13, 2020 - The Gift of Goodbye

It's called The Gift of Goodbye and it's an uncelebrated superpower. It enhances peace of mind, preserves heart health, and holds no space for conflict. Goodbye literally means God be with you... Goodness in parting. It's a well wish.

How divine is it to love from that space? To wish someone God when you part ways with them. The only thing that separates us from animals is our will...

Our ability to choose. Free will. If you don't choose me, I am still chosen. That's my spiritual reality. My emotional reality lines up with it.

Have you ever wondered why kissing me feels so good, and why it's hard to stop once we start? It's because I kiss you like it's going to be our last kiss. Even in our closeness is the gift of goodbye.

June 15, 2020 - Black Wolf

Black Wolf was a loner. Wolf Law mandated that wolves travel in packs to ensure survival. Black Wolf challenged that idea. He bet on himself and trusted himself to ensure his survival.

He understood the law of the land. He also knew how to hunt, protect, and defend. If survival was the objective, he didn't need a pack to achieve it. He had himself. They shunned him as an outlaw, not understanding that the law didn't apply to him.

"You act like you're above the law!!" they spewed with venom.

"I am the law," he calmly responded and carried on his way. It was hard for him to understand the social frustration with his individuality. He had observed the sheep. He studied their weaknesses. He observed the bear and recognized his strength. Survival was a simple mathematic equation. His survival wasn't threatened by the bear. They occupied two different lanes.

White Moon was the only one who understood him. She lifted him up. Occasionally she would summons him to the highest peak to bathe him in perspective. Inspiring him to howl "I am!!" Declaring himself to the world in a private celebration of individuality.

June 22, 2020 - The Pocket

In the world of percussion there is something called "The Pocket".

The pocket isn't a thought or idea. It can't be explained. It's an experience.

When you listen to a good drummer and feel a need to tap your foot or bob your head...

You are in the pocket. The pocket makes you move. It stimulates your spirit.

In African culture, the pocket is fine tuned. There's a drum for the movement of the feet, the core, and the upper body. The cadence of the drums enters the body and manifests dance.

The pocket is like love. When you vibe with someone it's the result of spiritual rhythm. When someone moves you the right way the rhythm is connecting with your soul.

The pocket gave birth to funk. It's the corner stone of what we call funk music. The pocket gave birth to individuality. Which is why we say, "He dances to the beat of his own drum."

That's the type of person you want to funk with.

June 22, 2020

Her background was the Blues. Imagine the soundtrack of an ugly divorce. She was evolving into a different genre of music. Jazz. She was jazzy.

Coming out of the blues she stood in her own light. The light of self-acceptance. It was a challenge for her to embrace her body. A full figure with perfect curves.
Weight issues had weighed her down. But here she stood. Representing herself naked and raw. Unfiltered and unafraid.

She told the blues to kiss her ass. Upholding her light, she announced herself to the world as I AM.

June 25, 2020 - The Switch

She was the type of woman that would ask you a question (she already knew the answer to) just see how you'd respond. She'd monitor your tone, your eyes, your body language. She was an investigator.

He understood this as a disobedient child. He knew how to lie because it was the only protection from the switch. The switch that he had to pick from the tree in the front yard. He tried to be clever and grab a skinny one. That pissed her off and she stomped to retrieve more. She whipped his ass.

In this moment, he grew to value discretion. The only way to avoid getting whipped was to avoid getting caught. But getting caught was inevitable. So was the switch.

This made him bold.

Lying felt cowardly. Sneaky. He learned the art of discretion. It became a guardian. It protected him from the switch.

His goal became to be a man. A man that didn't have to lie. A man who would tell it like it is. So when his lover began investigating... He smiled.

She asked him a question that she knew the answer to... he just smiled.

"Why are you laughing?"

Because you stimulate my inner child.

June 25, 2020 - The Joker

He operated from the assumption that Love was God. To love was to bless. Blessings were the response to prayer. He believed that it was his responsibility to show people God through the act of love. This made him special, but not special. There was a love letter in his heart for women. All women. He was fascinated by his mother's ability to raise 4 kids on her own. He idolized women. He celebrated women.

But his blessing was also a curse. An agent of God can't take anyone personally. He is obligated to honor his spirit and his spirit is programmed to uplift and enlighten.

How can a woman love a man who's calling exceeds the idea of marriage? For most women marriage is the ultimate goal of love. His goal was to enlighten. God gave him the story of a man that had been buried alive and lived to tell about it. In his story was inspiration for anyone who felt trapped, held back, oppressed. His life was a testimony. A love letter from God.

Such a man couldn't be taken personally, so he couldn't be taken seriously.

He was a joke...but no one was laughing.

June 28, 2020 - The Talk

She loved his words but hated the fact they weren't exclusive to her.

The conversation went...

"You talk the same way to all women. There's nothing exclusive about what you feel for me. You find beauty in all women. There's nothing special about it and I don't feel special."

He responded "Maybe you're not..."

"What the fuck does that mean? Are you saying that I'm not special?"

He explained with a smile..."Not at all. You said it! Quote: I don't feel special. That has nothing to do with me. If my actions don't make you feel special, maybe "special" wasn't there in the first place. That's not my business. I like you as you are. Sharing time with you is special. That's all I know."

He was impossible to talk to.

June 29, 2020 - Love Loss

The easiest way to accept losing someone is to love them completely while you have them.

If you lose at any game, you'll experience disappointment. But if you give your all, the pain of disappointment is far less than the pride of knowing that you gave your all.

The key is understanding that everyone has an expiration date. No one knows how they will lose someone.

Death and disagreement are inevitable circumstances. Sometimes people die. Other times, disagreements will lead to separation. Either way, giving your all is the remedy to love loss.

July 2, 2020 - Vegetarian

She was a well-practiced witch. Not prone to be a man eater. Instead, she turned men into vegetables. Much like Medusa turned men into stone.

He laid paralyzed by her love spell. Suffering the spiritual pain of being fully conscious but unable to move. He couldn't control himself. Literally. His brain couldn't reach his limbs.

But he was conscious. That's all he could be.

She had taken everything from him but his awareness.

He was aware of her sweet presence, but unable to respond...unable to express love.

She danced seductively in the moonlight of his darkest hour. Her silhouette was a perfect cascade of glitter and rain.

It wasn't her intent to torture him. She was just practicing her craft. Celebrating ancient rituals. Practicing them was the only way to keep them alive. This made her powerful, but dangerous. Drunk driving in a Ferrari. She was spiritually intoxicated and prone to crash a beautiful vehicle. Love.

It wasn't her fault that she understood karma and was sensitive to her past lives. She loved spirits not people. And his spirit was worthy of captivity. So she paralyzed him to preserve him for the next life

July 3, 2020 - Love & Fear

I can't imagine loving someone... at the same time... fearing that I'll lose them. That doesn't make sense to me. My brain isn't wired to function like that.

What's mine has always been mine. Rather it stays or comes and goes. The true gift of the human experience is time. That's the true value of life. We have this time to create, to evolve, and heal. I'd never spend my time holding on to someone out of fear and claim to love them.

To love is to serve. To love is to give time, willingly, with the intention of inspiring joy. Most of us only do this on birthdays or Christmas. For me, it's a lifestyle.

I'm highly aware of the gifts that come with me. I'm very intentional about the time I share with people. That time is a blessing. I don't take it for granted. Nor do I attach it to expectation. It's a gift that was given to me, thus I'm capable of giving it without fear of taking a loss.

July 3, 2020 - Narcissist

How dare you demonize the narcissist for providing the perfect mirror for you to see yourself. What is empathy without a host?

How dare you blame yourself for loving too fiercely, for believing too strongly, for hurting so deeply. He lost you and replaced you. Even that hurts. I encourage you to follow his lead. Let him go and replace him. Learn the lesson. He's a messenger.

If you demonize him, you hold on to the pain and position yourself as victim. If you celebrate him as a messenger, you take the lesson and move on with greater knowledge. Knowledge is power.

But you don't see the lesson because you can't see past your pain.

Do you think he is hurting? Absolutely not. Why? Because he loved you for a specific purpose. Once that purpose was served you no longer held value. I'm not concerned about the morality of his actions. I'm looking at the lesson. Is it wrong to love a person for a specific purpose? If I asked you why you want a man would you have a list of things based on your emotional needs? Of course. The difference, once you find what you're looking for you hold on... he moves on.

If you could let him go the way he let you go how liberating would that be?

Just a thought.

July 5, 2020 - Her Memes

Her memes were sometimes humorous, other times deep, always provocative.

She tickled his intelligence. He found himself smiling with morning coffee anticipating her posts. She never disappointed. A consistent source of joy.

She noticed him noticing her. They began commenting on each other's posts. Harmless social media banter that became flirting. Mutual friends took notice.

They asked her, "How do you know him?"

She laughed and replied, "He's a FB friend."

They found no humor in how she responded and issued a firm warning "Don't go there! He's dangerous. We've never seen him out with the same woman twice!!" She wasn't put off by their observation. She had already studied him. She had picked him apart and saw herself in his reflection. She couldn't look away...despite red flags.

July 5, 2020 - Red Flags

He had developed a reputation for being scandalous because he gave no effort to fit in. He disregarded social norms and viewed most people as sheep. Slaves to unquestioned values.

He had grown to not care about social opinions. Criticisms of his character only fueled his rugged individualism.

In the arena of love, he was a lover. In the arena of art, he was an artist. His mediums of expression would shift according to his will. He was a follower of spirit and lover of life.

For most of his life he was in a cage. Freedom was in his trinity of values.

Health, Wealth, and Freedom.

Loving him was a challenge because his love came from spirit, not social construct. He would throw red flags on purpose because it was exhausting to break hearts. He knew that only a certain type of woman would understand his emotional world view. The unicorn.

She wouldn't be deterred by red flags. They would be the same red flags she used to ward off men she knew couldn't handle the ride.

July 7, 2020 - Head Game

It started with his bald head and beard. It ended with his eyes and the sound of his voice. She became fixated with his mouth. The structure of his lips. The way he spoke English with a slightly southern accent.

She said "I'm a straight shooter and I don't like wasting time. You are the perfect person to have an affair with. You're discreet and your confidence intrigues me. I think it's bullshit.

In my younger years I would break you down, chew you up, and spit you out. Just because you look like fun. Your mouth tells me everything I need to know about a night with you. But I can't betray my husband by satisfying my curiosity. However, I'm too invested in my imagination to let you off the hook. So here's my proposal. You charge $90 an hour for a massage. I'm going to deposit $500 in your account for two hours of your time and book the room. What do you think?"

He smiled.

"I think... Either you think too much of yourself, or too little of me." as he slowly licked the salt off the margarita rim and proposed a toast to their last conversation.

July 7, 2020 - Gifts

There is no need to chase a gift.

Gifts arrive in our lives for the purpose of being unwrapped and enjoyed. That's all.

Anything else is game.

If you know that you are a gift...give yourself.

If you think you're a gift and position yourself for a chase, you'll become an acquisition. Something to be earned through strategy.

Man is a hunter. We are programmed to perform a mating dance. We will bite the bait.

Keep in mind that all chases come to an end. But gifts are built to keep giving. Thus, the phrase "The gift that keeps on giving."

July 7, 2020 - Spoiler Alert

I love how I want to be loved. Too me... love equals freedom.

If my freedom offends our relationship, your possession will offend my individuality. Then the relationship becomes toxic.

There is nothing you can do with another man that will have the power to offend me. I respect you as the owner of yourself. I trust you to govern yourself. That's all. And that is what makes our time together so special. It's seasoned with choice. It's intentional.

When we are together, we are consciously choosing one another. Anything else is generic.

Nuff said.

July 7, 2020 - Ghost

She had suffered so many lames that she had grown to devalue men. This made her a well packaged "thirst trap". It was an unconscious dynamic. She'd pull you in just to measure your thirst... Only to discard you once you expressed too much interest.

It was set in her mind that men couldn't handle her. She needed to be tamed, not loved. Conquered not romanced.

Her appearance was striking but her demeanor was standoffish. Most men who were bold enough to approach her fit into a certain category. Dogs. They only wanted sex. She did too. She just wasn't honest about it. There was an obstacle course on the path to her presence. Put in place to measure your character. Your thirst. But he wasn't thirsty.

He came to the table as a tall glass of water. His mode of operation threw her off balanced. She needed him to make a move on her so she could reject his advances. He didn't.

This confused her. So rather than play hard to get she made herself fully available...

And he made himself disappear.

July 9, 2020 - Empathy

"He sacrificed his only begotten love, to save the world".
- The Book of Sol

You don't know it, but I empathize with you. I, too, have fallen in love with a poet. I know what it feels like to read her words and wonder if she's talking to me, about me...

I know what it feels like to want to be someone's sole inspiration.

Just as you lost me, I lost her. I lost her to herself. Which means she was never mine. She never belonged to me. I celebrate that. When I met her, I knew that she belonged to the world. I knew that she was in love with the moon and her mind channeled messages from the universe. She was a vehicle. To take her personally would rob the world of the gift God created her to be.

Our relationship was cosmic. More Big Bang than "happily ever after."

Our relationship was created to create...not sustain.

Imagine an orgasm in comparison to the process of courtship.

July 10, 2020 - Kissing

I have fantasies about kissing you.

In my mind, I kiss you with my eyes open. Aware of how sacred your privacy is. Conscious to file each moment as a memory.

I want to own your mouth.

Have you ever loved a soldier?

Have you ever felt the embrace of a man who returned from war?

Have you ever felt a kiss that says "I miss you, need you, adore you...and I'm glad that you exist."

My kiss is a perfect blend of lust and spirituality. Connection and deliverance. I kiss you with the intention of setting a standard. Raising the bar.

When you return to your person, I want you to feel something missing from the relationship. With my kiss comes awareness and liberation.

I have abandonment issues so I kiss you in a way that guarantees you'll want to kiss me again.

I have fantasies about kissing you...

July 12, 2020 - Jada

The social hypocrisy around this woman is amazing. I don't mind people judging open relationships. But I've seen women demonize her as a child abuser. With all the conversation about narcissists and empaths in the air, it seems like we'd be more compassionate towards someone who clearly reminds us of ourselves.

If you've never felt compelled to heal someone perhaps you can't relate to the dynamic. And perhaps you should reevaluate your idea of love.

It's cause and effect. What she experienced is the reason why doctors, therapists, and pastors have rule books. Safeguards are in place to ensure clear boundaries. There are no such rules for lovers. Love is not a profession.

Lovers are more spiritual than logical. We are prone to experience the feeling of a thing even if our mind thinks it's wrong. Have you never loved the wrong person? Have you never felt the sweet passion of an emotional indiscretion? Gtfoh!

The funny thing is this...

It's old news to all parties involved. She and Will are still family. They healed the situation. They have victory. It seems we'd want to celebrate that... But who am I to judge?

July 12, 2020

She mounted him with the intention of consuming his seed. Sex with him was always about her. He would sponsor multiple orgasms and never allow himself to cum. She was tired of it. She wanted to hear him roar and feel him explode inside of her walls.

She mounted him with purpose, gyrating her hips to inspire maximum penetration. She wanted all of him and wouldn't stop until she got it. She fucked him slow and kissed him with passion. Encouraging him to let go. Speaking to him in body language. But he wouldn't release his discipline. His focus was always energy.

Always the bigger picture. Sex for him was about magic. He didn't need to cum to perform magic. Sex was about healing and release...elevation and exaltation...The experience of oneness.

She was missing the point.

It wasn't about coming. It was about arriving. Being totally present and understanding that the body houses a spirit. His desire was to stimulate the spirit within and bring it without. There was no need for him to cum... he was already there. Fully present.

July 13, 2020

He was an oral historian who spoke fluent body language. He understood that there was light within her flesh. A light he was designed to turn on. His kisses were paragraphs of divine reflection. He understood that sexual trauma had stunted her feminine growth. She was still that young girl, disguised as a vibrant woman. His mission was to kiss her privacy in a way that spoke to her soul. Her essence.

He couldn't preach to her about the beauty of freedom and the power of forgiveness.

"Why me?" Was a slogan that echoed through her vibration. The childhood trauma changed her composition and he sought to realign her with the perfection God created her from. She had been to therapy. She had talked it through. Still, "Why me?" was a consistent theme of her internal dialogue.

His method of healing was simple. He provided an atmosphere of deep trust and unconditional love. In his presence she could feel nothing but love and see nothing but light. His kisses changed her narrative. His tongue wrote a love letter in her folds. He told her a story about herself that took down her guard and allowed light to burst from her darkness. She saw the light because she was the light.

July 14, 2020 - Cheating

Cheating is heartless. It implies that one doesn't have the courage to stand in their own truth.

I'd much rather tell you what it is from the beginning so you can make an informed decision. I'm not one to think that everyone is for everybody. Nor do I think that emotional appetites stay the same. I've been the sounding board for too many wives. Things change in relationships because people change. I'm ok with that reality.

I also understand the appeal of cheating. The fun of it. The danger attached to it. After all, God gave us access to all the trees except one. And which one did we choose? The forbidden tree. Human natural is wired that way. I don't hold us to unreal expectations.

The idea of cheating is beneath my character. Sex is only magical when it's seasoned with consciousness. I'm not a man who could sleep with a drunk woman. That's too close to rape. If her mind isn't fully there, neither am I. Choice is necessary.

To deceive...is to "make believe". I'm not into fairy tales. Nor am I a fan of intoxicating women with deception. I need you to know exactly who I am because my individuality is one of my best qualities. The choice is yours.

July 14, 2020 - Twos-Day

She had him...and him.

One of them was an artist in the bedroom and an emotional guide. The other was a space filler. One served a purpose at home, the other satisfied her need to socialize and be courted. One of them took her for granted. The other one didn't. Yet both benefited from each other.

If she needed to get away from the frustrations at home, she had a safe place to get away.

The one at home was happy to see her go. He understood that sometimes being too close can be a bad thing. Distance serves it purpose.

The getaway understood that when she called it was his time to show up. And since their time was so limited he'd always show up in a big way. She needed that. He needed that.

So did the other. It worked for them all.

She wasn't as stressed because she had an exhaust valve in both situations. If home made her frustrated, the getaway released it. He served his purpose. The other served his place.

July 15, 2020 - Toxic

I want a relationship, but I don't want a relationship.

Well... I want someone but I don't want to belong to anyone. I mean...we can be cool. Like, cool, cool. But labels make me cringe. They remind me of prison. I want you close but I never want to be trapped in your expectations. I'll disappoint you every time.

My deepest need is to be free. Not loved. Love is a natural occurrence in my life. I carry it with me everywhere I go. And because I am free, I value time. I cherish every second of life. A moment with you is equal to a moment without you. I understand the Bible when it says, "God is not a respecter of persons." Neither am I. Everyone is divine.

In your mind, the experience of deep love is attached to the idea of monogamy.

Well…

Keep your pussy and how it feels, I'd rather feel your spirit and how it heals.

July 15, 2020 - BeWitched

She raised his kundalini while praying to his temple. As a Christian blesses the table before eating, she blessed his body in the process of consuming erection. She loved him in a dangerous way. The only way, for love is submission.

She seduced him with Reiki and took him to another sexual plane. She granted his wish for a threesome as she invited her Spirit Guide to their love session. Bringing him to brink of climax, she retrieved the candle from her shrine and poured three ceremonial drops on his navel. She blessed the last place he was connected to his mother.

Holding his torso in place she pulled him into the deepest aspect of her kiss. She swallowed him whole and hummed a mantra of thanksgiving. Using his erection as a tuning rod she connected him to his source. Goose bumps covered her flesh as she tasted his glowing aura. He arrived speaking in tongues.

She savored the sweet taste of victory.

July 16, 2020

It was his version of an unfiltered selfie. His darkness coexisted with his light. There was no war. Each served a purpose. Self-knowledge made him grounded. He could mingle amongst witches and Christians alike. He found Christians to be interesting. They held a high capacity of judgment towards the witches. "Those women are demonic. They practice witchcraft."

"So what...you do the same," he continued "You drink wine as a symbol for blood and eat crackers as a symbol for flesh? How can you judge someone else's communion?"

Oneness has no place for judgment. When you see yourself in the other, you see God in all.

But un-wholly people radiate division. It's starts with the "me against myself" and it ends up projected onto the world.

July 16, 2020 - The Bad Guy

As a kid he was prone to danger. When playing cops and robbers, he was always the bad guy. He wanted to be the one that broke rules and got away.

As a man, this tendency lingered. He didn't mind taking a risk. Taking chances made him feel alive. Humans are most aware when in the presence of danger. He lived a conscious lifestyle so danger came with it.

He was too bright for his own good. He had the capacity to justify any transgression. The type of man who'd do the wrong thing for the right reason. This is why she loved him. He didn't give a fuck. He was raw and undomesticated. All her rules and barriers meant nothing to him...So they lost value to her.

His lack of regard was contagious. She found herself free for the first time in a long time. Free of self-criticism, past conditionings, and social judgments. This made her wet.

Where there is moisture, there is receptivity. So he didn't have to ask, she gave willingly. There's a reason why the superhero is always nerdy and the villain is sexy.

He had no desire to save the day. Instead, he saved the moments that made the story worth watching. His passion was criminal. A paint brush designed to blur lines and escape the consequences. He sponsored secret memories that were worthy of fantasy and self-gratification. It was his nature.

July 19, 2020 - Making Up

He lost consciousness in the taste of her neck. A passion mark was the result. He forgot about the rules of suction. She had him in the doghouse for two weeks. Starving him of her presence. Once she broke down and let him out, he attacked.

It was inevitable. He had suffered the loss of her. This time...she was serious about leaving him. So, this time...he was obsessed to make her stay.

She wasn't the type of woman to be loose with her body. He used this to his advantage. He knew that she needed him as much as he needed her. In that way.

After a few texts he invited her out for dinner. Her favorite spot. She accepted. Knowing he hadn't changed. Knowing he'd repeat the same mistakes and hurt her again. Still...she accepted.

He knew her patterns. Her tendency to wash her hands before being seated. So, when she arrived and went to the ladies' room, he locked the door behind her. She turned in surprise. He went straight for the jugular. There was nothing to say. No apologies needed.

His apologies always ended up making her explore higher levels of orgasm. This is why she loved him. Loved him knowing that he'd give her a reason to break up again...and recreate another version of this moment.

July 22, 2020 - Yogini

You never shun organized religion. Your spirituality embraces all. You understand western thought but you think from an eastern perspective. Your heart is so kind that it would be easy for someone to take advantage of you.

But no one can take from a person who'd willingly surrender.

You value energy, not possessions. Time, not things.

That's why you are protected from evil. You taste like righteousness and smell like fresh rain.

Your aura radiates sexuality because you are so intimately involved in life. You dance, you sing, you breathe deeply and stretch. You feel good about "you" and people feel good around you. Your presence inspires my faith in humanity.

Thank you for existing.

July 22, 2020 - Blessings

You've been waiting on a man who speaks your language, so why are you pausing. Do you think that you have time to spare? Why resist? Play coy. The hour is passing you by. Have you played so many games with men that you've grown to think that game is a part of the play....the courtship?

I can't explain it to you but I assure you it's not. On a spiritual level, you are a treasure. Treasures are discovered. You've had enough secular experiences to know that you're spiritual. You've done your inner work.

So why are you waiting? Why are you wasting precious time. Do you not trust the God you claim to pray to? Do you not believe in blessings.

God is the father as you are a parent. You know the feeling of blessing your child with something they need. When they express appreciation, it makes it much easier to bless them again. If they show disregard, well... You're less prone to bless them again.

Make sure you're on the right side of history babe. God is watching.

July 23, 2020 - Half Hippie, Half Hood'

Her shirt read "Half hippie half hood"...

He had no reference for the blend of those concepts. He understood the hood. But the hippie part was a mystery. His quest for understanding led him deep in the woods on a quest to nowhere. A thunderstorm approached and it began to rain. He sought shelter. She did the opposite. Taking her shoes off she darted into the storm beyond the cover of trees.

Lifting her head to the sky, she closed her eyes and opened her arms as if embracing the atmosphere. Her bohemian sundress clung to her skin as her hips swayed from side to side. Seductively dancing to a music he couldn't hear.

"Come!!" She yelled towards him. "Don't be a pussy! Come feel the earth under your feet and the rain on your skin. Mother Earth is celebrating. The farmers are rejoicing."

As he approached her, she began taking off her dress as she danced. Tossing the wet fabric aside she held his hands and motioned for him to groove. "Loosen up. Feel the vibe."

He gave in to the movement and instinctively made himself naked. He felt his ego die as his animal self-joined forces with his higher self.

"That's what I'm talking about" she said with a wink and a smile.

She embraced him. They became one flesh. She kissed his third eye and whispered in his ear while fondling his erection. She explained that it was a season of fertility and the earth needed his seed. It was the perfect time for manifestation. She told him to set an intention and plant it. Promising him she would help co-create his dream. Then she became the earth. The seed was planted and nurtured...in nature.

July 24, 2020 - Black/White

Sweetheart don't be confused. I'm not being heartless. I just don't care to entertain emotions that aren't beneficial to our evolution. I, unlike you, know how precious time is.

I also understand that what you focus on expands. So why be at odds with someone I love?

I agree with you. Sometimes I can be an asshole. So what? I don't expect you to like me all the time. Sometimes you will hate me, dislike me, resent me.... So what?

Love is our foundation. "Like" is its branches. Branches are prone to the wind. A storm can blow branches away. But the tree still stands. Your attitude is a branch. Your mood is a branch. The right amount of wind will blow them both away. But the tree will still stand.

So it's not that I'm heartless and don't care about your feelings. I just know that our foundation is love. And love doesn't fold to the wind. You can feel whatever you want. But the only feeling, worth feeling, is love.

Love is my focus, my commitment, my agreement. Nothing else matters. If it doesn't heal us, it doesn't build us. It's as simple as that.

Conflict negates connection. And you know me... Connecting is what I'm good at.

July 24, 2020 - Presence

When you lose your life to prison, survive, and come home with a sound mind, certain things lose value. Like noise. The sound of opinions and perceptions.

The sound of dysfunction and narrowmindedness.

When you have escaped the ever-present noise of the cell block, you search the world for a song. People who sing. People who have bars (the ability to articulate themselves). You seek intelligence and harmony. Righteousness and wise allies.

When you've had your future taken from you it teaches you to absorb the moment. The power of being fully present and leaving nothing behind. But society operates from a different paradigm. People are present in the moment but thinking about the future. Everyone misses the now. People work to pay bills. Their work is attached to the future.

I'm blessed to be able to find great joy in my work and get paid for it. But the pay isn't the reward. The work is. I'm in the business of making people better. The reward is in being present, as a present, with the gifts God gave me.

July 26, 2020 - Game

It was an official date with an unspoken invite to her bedroom. He had pursued her vigorously and she enjoyed his attention. So much so, she wasn't done playing with him yet.

They drank wine on her Victorian sofa, laughed, and totally ignored the Netflix movie they had set out to watch.

They were truly into each other and the conversation eventually turned sexual. She used it as an opportunity to prolong the inevitable. The decision had already been made...She was going to sleep with him. But not yet. She was enjoying the chase. Even though the chase was over.

They spoke about their sexual ambitions. Things they liked to give and receive. She introduced an erotic craving that caused him to burst out in nervous laughter.

"Nah... I'm not into that. You're crazy. That's gay."

He bit the bait. The game could be extended.

"What's gay about it?" she questioned, and continued... "If you know you're a man you wouldn't say something like that. If you find my sexual appetite forbidden that means you've never explored your whole body. Which means that you can't possibly know what you are or what's gay."

"Shiiiid... I didn't have to smoke crack to know it'll fuck your life up. I'm cool on all of that babe. Let's finish the movie. I have to get home so I can get ready for work in the morning".

End game.

July 27, 2020 - Flatline

They had a thing for each other. A thing that never ended. She had been in two relationships during their amour. He was a loyal go-to guy...a side piece. Comfortable in his position he knew he could only have her a few hours each week. That was fine. Then her man told her to stop seeing him. He wasn't comfortable with their "friendship". She ended it with tears in her eyes.

The next day flowers showed up at her job. A dozen of bright red roses with a note that read, "Thank you for making me feel special." signed "Yours".

She rushed home after work, cleaned the house, and cooked a gourmet dinner. She lit candles in the bedroom and adorned herself in a negligée hidden by her favorite robe. Anticipating that he'd be tired after work she blended an energy drink into his smoothie. She had plans for him.

As expected, he came home tired, ate, and was ready for bed. He failed to notice her make up or the effort she put into the meal and the atmosphere. He showered and was toweling off when she entered the bathroom, opened her robe, and posed seductively in the doorway. She escorted him to the bedroom and gave him the business. He didn't have to do anything but lay there. He came out of his sex coma smiling as she gazed in his eyes. Knowing she had turned it up a few notches he asked, "What was that for babe?"

She said, "Because the flowers you sent made me feel like a queen."

"What flowers?" he asked.

Flatline...

July 27, 2020 - Healing

I saw a post that asked, "How long should it take to heal in between relationships?" The responses baffled me. The post baffled me. My mind doesn't work that way or ask those kinds of questions.

Healing is not a matter of time; it's a state of mind. Healing involves acceptance of reality. If a woman leaves me, there are two perceptions. There's the pain of her absence and the joy of my presence. I choose me every time. In choosing joy, I celebrate the time we've shared and the lessons we've learned. The experience was a blessing.

I accept the reality that people have a right to change their minds. Human appetites change.

No harm in that. But there's great harm in holding on to someone who's moved on. It's dangerous. Masochistic. Lovers hurt each other over those type of feelings. A healed individual can have a healthy relationship... even when it ends.

It begins with self and comes with self. The loss of a lover can't change my internal reality. I'm well and I wish you well. Simple as that. No extended goodbyes. No wishes for a return. Thus, no need to take time to heal. Healing is in the hello, as well as the letting go.

July 28, 2020 - The Bottom Line

She asked me how to stop mourning the loss of her boyfriend, so we did a "cost benefit analysis" - a well-known business practice. We broke the relationship down to assets and liabilities. His liability section far outweighed his assets. He didn't make her feel seen, loved, valued, or protected. In fact, his only asset was sex. It wasn't that the sex was so good.

She was just a monogamous-minded woman who attached sex to the idea of commitment. When she opened her legs she opened her heart. That was her mistake. She thought that sex meant commitment. And the idea of commitment was associated with her personal experience, not his. She didn't work that out in the beginning. She assumed that he'd line up with her emotional worldview if she submitted her body to him.

After seeing the math of the relationship on paper she realized that she was mourning the idea, not the reality. She didn't really miss him. She missed the idea of him. The reality of his presence was more a liability than an asset. In any business it feels good to release liabilities and employ assets.

The love business is no different. Your presence is your company. Successful companies know how to hire and manage people who are assets. The loss of liabilities increases the bottom line.

July 29, 2020 - Avocado

She was holistic and vegan. Her morning ritual involved meditation and yoga. Afterwards she'd eat a raw avocado. Slicing it in half with the blade, she'd remove the top half exposing the seed lodged in the other. Usually, she'd stab the large seed with the knife, twist it, and dislodge it. But this morning he stopped her. He held it in his hands, studied it, and told her how it resembled a vagina. Raising it to his opened mouth, his teeth locked around the seed as his lips pressed against the raw green flesh. His tongue served as a knife to loosen it. He popped it out and let it fall to the floor. He looked at her without saying a word.

She understood. He wanted suck out her seed.

Her morning ritual was a source of arousal. There's nothing more sexy than a woman who makes space for God and wellness in the beginning of her day. A woman who sets the tone of her day with specific intentions.

He proceeded to ravish the raw avocado from its firm, dark, skin. He chewed into the buttery interior until it was gone. Leaving behind traces in his beard as he licked his lips and looked her in the eyes. "Damn!" She whispered under her breathe as she dropped the knife to the floor...along with her yoga pants.

July 20, 2020 - Open Relationship

You couldn't call it an "open relationship"...it was a relationship that was open. By design. An intimate friendship that had no ending. He trained her to keep her distance but encouraged her to remain close.

She met him as a socialite. A social light that enjoyed sharing his light with the world.

He knew things. Spiritual things. His story was written by God and he was gifted to tell it. He belonged to the world. She understood that. Yet somehow, she belonged to him.

Every time she wanted to let go, she realized there was no reason to. He offered a particular kind of feel good that's rare in this society. He saw everything through the eyes of gratitude, which naturally made people more thankful for the blessings in their lives. Which naturally made him attractive. Someone you gravitate towards.

He welcomed her to men, understanding the importance of feeling attractive. He was her friend, lover, and guide. He had no interest in courting her. That's where men could serve a purpose in her life. A void he left open for the taking.

So it wasn't an "open relationship"... It was a relationship that was open.

August 2, 2020 - Addiction

He was becoming a habit-forming drug. Rather she took him orally or by injection he had the ability to remove her pain and empower her to function without discomfort. She was beginning to need him. If she went too long without him, she'd experience the violent symptoms of withdrawal. She didn't realize it until it was too late. He was in her bloodstream.

Closely associated with her nerve endings, his only purpose was to make her feel better, which ultimately made her feel worse when she didn't have him.

He was a natural anti-depressant. She knew the dangers of becoming attached to him so she gave effort to maintain a certain distance. The more distance between them, the more she wanted him. Each painful step away from him only reminded her of the beauty of having him inside her. It wasn't healthy but it felt good.

She embraced the long-term consequences of her addiction. It was better to have him in her system than not. He was a habit she cared not to recover from. Even if she hit rock bottom, he'd be there to heal her wounds and take away her pain. So, she continued to use him. Careful not to abuse him. Taking him in moderate doses... as needed. She knew that she was hooked, but if she could exercise a bit of control over him she could pretend otherwise.

Addiction has a way of seducing us into being co-creators of its reality...

August 2, 2020 - Cold World

If having your heart broken can turn you cold, then having proper love can make you hot. If you have lost your receptivity to love, then being cold is the choice for your reality.

Don't expect a man to change your mind. The man wants access to your heart. If your heart is forbidden so is the opportunity to warm up and heal.

Your coldness is a product of fear. Your fear is a product of pain. Have you ever looked at that and questioned why you'd hold on to something that's toxic...something that doesn't serve you? It repeats itself each day. It re-creates itself each day but only with your permission and assistance.

Deeper than that, holding on to past pain means you're holding on to the man who hurt you. So you're not really single, you're on ice with the man who broke your heart.

... Cold world

August 2, 2020 - Sacrifice

She had lived too long in her own mind. Keeping things to herself. Bottled up. Unable to express. Unwilling to be free. Her mind was a refuge. Even her concept of spirituality was a mental construct. An idea, not a practiced energy. However, she was evolving, and with her evolution came him.

She knew him before she met him. Something about him was familiar to her spirit. He moved her. Stirred her insides from a distance. As a stranger. If he could affect her from a distance, she knew what would happen if she got close to him. Remember...She lived in her mind, so her imagination had already ran wild with possibilities. More sexual than she was willing to admit, her mind revealed her as a slut for passion. She saw herself with him in ways she hadn't entertained with other men.

She found herself giving in to the desire to know him. She opened the line of communication and made herself available for an adventure. Fuck it. The worst that could happen is they'd meet and the chemistry wouldn't be there. She was curious enough to find out.

They exchanged messages and she privately cheered for his success.

"Please don't fuck this up by sending a dick pic!" She laughed in thought.

He didn't. In fact, he did the opposite. He said all of the right things and put actions behind his words. Refreshing, yet dangerous. He had the power to compel her. Pull her out of her shell. He had eyes...he saw her. She wanted to be seen. Naked. Unafraid. It felt like she was becoming a willing sacrifice, but really, she was sacrificing her walls for freedom. Losing her mind to gain the experience of spiritual love.

August 3, 2020 - Pain

He was into pain. The kind of pain that comes with the perfect pressure of a deep tissue massage or a good workout. Positive pain. The kind that reminds you that you've done the work, or had the work done to you. Pain you want to run from but you embrace because it's healthy. He wasn't shy about his desire to push boundaries and test limitations. He understood the natural process of growth. It's painful. It stretches you. Makes you stronger. This made him attractive to her.

She, too, had a thing for pain. She had lived with it for most of her life. She carried unhealed wounds of past lovers which gave her a veneer of toughness. Her strength was an illusion. She had become emotionally lazy...Unfit...

Out of shape, because she hadn't exercised her heart in a while.

He was the right trainer for her dilemma. He pushed her buttons without being afraid of her response. He pissed her off in the process pushing past her limitations.

He didn't care if she quit, the session was already paid for by God. And if she tried to quit, he knew the right words to say to challenge her ego to do more.

His faith in her potential exceeded her self-doubt. Providing a space for her heart to race. Increasing her blood flow. Making her breathe hard and sweat.

The pleasure of the pain he caused her expanded her womanhood. It broadened her perception of what she could or couldn't do. It made her more capable, more powerful, more alive...

August 6, 2020 - Abuse

If a man punches you in the face for running your mouth...the next time you run your mouth you know exactly what to expect. So if you stay with him, you are choosing a life where your voice doesn't matter. Swallowing your relevance will come with a path of eggshells. You'll walk on them extremely mindful not to complain for the rest of your life with him. You will only have the right to remain silent under the constant threat of punishment.

If a man controls your voice, he controls your soul. You will do anything he tells you to do. But then again... You're the one who so proudly says "I'll do anything for him."

I see now.

Message to a friend.

August 8, 2020 - Happily

It's embarrassing to love someone more than they love you. If you commit your "all" to a fraction there will always be something missing in the equation. Validation will be missing. Reflection will be missing.

A fraction can't mirror a whole, as 50 can't balance 100. It's impossible. But the good news is, if you're dating in your 40's you have the opportunity to create balance. If you have survived the divorce and the kids are grown, you now have the freedom to choose love on your terms. The idea of happily ever after was an illusion. You know this now. So even though "ever after" is gone you still have the "happily" to hold on to. Happily is achieved by loving him the way he loves you. Meeting him where he's at and selfishly engaging the parts of him that are available. Yet, keeping your options open. This doesn't make you lose. It makes you free.

You once thought that you could have everything you wanted in one man. That's no longer the case. You're empowered to have multiple streams of emotional income. Why settle for anything less? You've spent 20 years in a serious relationship. How did that work out? It didn't. So give yourself permission to have fun.

This is the time for you to explore your sexuality and unlock repressed aspects of your womanhood. This is the time to venture your erotic imagination and experience the taboo. You are no longer restrained by the hoax of monogamy. You now have the power to select partners who stimulate your spirit and inspire curiosity. You now have the power to experience a journey without the anxiety of reaching a certain destination. The "ever after" doesn't exist, but "happily" resides in the moment, the choice, the situation. Embrace it. You deserve it.

August 9, 2020 - On Love

Love is the healthiest of human exercises. It stimulates the heart and increases cardio. It strengthens the core and increases emotional endurance. It's no mystery why people who love hard are the most vulnerable to pain. Nor is it a question why good sex is called love making. Both parties are giving the same effort with the same purpose. Connecting...Giving of self. Seeking nothing in return but the pleasure of the partner.

Fresh love is the best. When the object of affection has access to your imagination. Nothing equals the pleasure of overcoming a lover's guard. Figuring out what makes them tick and finding ways to conquer them. Love without seduction is bland. Resistance is necessary for seduction to take place. Obstacles are necessary.

Damaged women create the atmosphere for the best love affairs. Weak men don't have the bandwidth to endure the challenge of capturing them. Men have made it easy for her to place "all men" in a box. That's why the one who stands out, stands up. Becomes erect. Inspires moisture and receptivity. His energy has the capacity to turn her on. Only then can she be worked out.

August 10, 2020 - WTF

She was a candid creature. A woman who knew the value of time. She told him that she wasn't looking for anything serious so don't catch feelings. Fair enough. She was an empty nester figuring herself out. Exploring her sexuality and selfishly seeking pleasure. Having fun. Nothing serious.

He was supposed to be her "flavor of the week", but the week turned into a month. When she had free time, she wanted to spend it with him. Over and over again. It became a cause for concern. Was she catching feelings?

Nahhh... She was just having fun.

She started questioning why he was always her choice. He made her realize that she wanted more than fun. She wanted to be seen... involved. He engaged her mind and there was nothing they couldn't talk about. Never a judgment. Always a thoughtful response. She could tell him the scandalous details of her dating life and he'd stand in full support of her freedom. Offering the male perspective to sharpen her game. She loved him for that.

Every time his advice panned out, she'd fall deeper in love. Until it was too late. She was caught up. Unable to deny her feelings and unable to voice them. Love put her in a chokehold. She had established the rules in the beginning. Nothing serious.

This shit was not supposed to be happening. WTF?

August 11, 2020 - The Practice

I'm too deep to be shallow. Your surface is only appealing to my eyes. I live from my heart which means I'll get under your skin. I'll push your buttons. The good and the bad. I'll piss you off and magically transform that anger into passion. Manifested as an eager embrace and oral collision.

A good chess player can announce his moves knowing that you lack the power to stop him.

I will flex my emotional intelligence and impose my will on you. After all, that's what you quietly desire. To be taken. You've been desensitized by male attention. Too many "Hey Beautifull's" and "You're gorgeous". Your appearance has become a burden. You're too attractive. But like most women, you're prone to give more credit to your flaws. You can easily spot beauty in other women but not so much yourself. You know that you're easy on the eyes, you just don't want to be praised as such. Thus, my disregard for your beauty is appealing. My investigation of your interior is stimulating. You open yourself out of impulse and curiosity. The seed is already planted. You like how I feel inside of you.

As I told you in beginning... Sex isn't the goal, it's the practice.

August 11, 2020 - Being Used

Let me play devil's advocate for a minute. Your way of thinking isn't uncommon. You think he is using you, right? So, let me ask... is that a bad thing?

The reason you think he's using you is because you have been used before. Played for your value. Now you are guarded. Skeptical of man's intentions. That's what happens when "use" becomes "abuse". However, underneath the pain of being abused is a desire to be used.

Ripe fruit will die on the tree if not picked and consumed. You know your value to man. What good is that value if it's not given? In the social arena we gain education in a particular field to make ourselves a value to the market. We get hired and paid based on our capabilities... Our ability to add our value to the company.

It's no different in relationships. Your value enhances his company. If you withhold your value, there is no growth. Being used is not a bad thing. It's a necessary ingredient of success. Being abused is bad. No one should suffer abuse. Yet it's one of life's greatest teachers. If it teaches you to be fearful and guarded, you'll be like a great lover who has no one to love. You'll possess the skill of passion without a host. That's a form of hell.

Ask yourself what he wants from you and imagine how it feels to give it. Does he possess a character worthy of your treasure? Is his love worth the calculated risk you're willing to take on his behalf? Would lifting him up make you feel uplifted. If not, abort the mission and save yourself some time. If so, give yourself and experience the pleasure of being useful to someone who values you.

It's not about living in the fear of being used. It's about being used by someone who appreciates what you have to give. That's the key.

August 12, 2020

You know that I'm not a fan of make-up, but tonight I want you to adorn a heavy smokey eye. The darker and bolder the better. I want you to doll up in your provocative gear, look yourself in the mirror, and give her a powerful name. Bring her to me with an opened mind.

Tonight, we are going to visit your trauma. We are going to confront the men who assaulted your inner child. We are going to be bold and have a candid conversation with them. I'll hold your hand as you tell them how their abuse changed your perspective of men and how they effected your coming relationships. I want to see your rage transform into forgiveness as you recognize the futility of holding on to their transgressions. I want you to experience the full extent of your anger, only then will you recognize it as a cage. Only then will you set yourself free.

We will perform a ritual. A burning ceremony. We will violently throw wine glasses in the fireplace and release toxic emotions. We will set fire to memories that no longer serve you. Let that shit go...

I will behold you as a new woman. Healed in the presence of my love. Your smokey eyes will be smeared by tears of liberation. Your face will be a mess but your heart will be whole, free. I'll wash your face gently. Symbolizing the removal of a mask. There will be no need to pretend. No need to be made up...nothing to hide behind...no flaws to cover up. My healing touch will make your skin glow naturally. I'm certain that once you see your clear reflection you will rejoice. When you look yourself in the eyes without the dark shadow of trauma you will never be the same. You will be reborn. Your face will radiate self-love and freedom.

My purpose will be served. Tonight, we are going to practice healing.

August 13, 2020 - Masochist

I wish that you could hear me from my perspective without imposing your perception. I guess no one has told you this, but you see things from pain. The possibility of pain shadows your every thought. You've gotten good at anticipating it so that you can avoid it. You're excellent at spotting all the signs, which are also signs of pleasure. But the outcome is how you frame it.

You are foolish enough to guard yourself from something good because you anticipate something bad. Even more foolishly, you've grown to take pride in your defense mechanism, not aware that you are defending yourself from something good.

No man will ever line up with your idea of relationship. You tailor it that way. You uphold yourself as someone who won't compromise her standards, yet it is you who is compromising your own happiness with your way of thinking. Men have made you feel so bad that you have assumed a superior disposition. Beyond pain. Untouchable. Unlovable. And it all stems from you. You are the orchestrator of the reality.

When you finally open up and become vulnerable, I'm sure you will find a perfect reflection in a man who hurts you as much as you hurt yourself. It can be no other way. You will ultimately prove yourself right...even if you're wrong.

August 18, 2020 - Falling Back

There's a difference between ghosting and falling back. I didn't ghost you. I simply fell back because I don't make a habit of wasting time. At this point in life, you are unlovable. You are not really single because you're in a relationship with your assumptions. Your first assumption is that all men want is sex. So the time we shared wasn't quality time. It wasn't about US...connecting. It was about you calculating my moves trying to fit me into some imaginary mold that you have in your mind. That's a turn off.

Your second assumption is that pussy is worth more than dick. So you set the stage for a man to chase you. I don't chase. Again, it's a waste of time. You can hold your pussy for ransom all you want. You dangle it like a carrot on a stick, until a whim hits you and you catch enough feelings to allow sexual connection. That's bizarre.

So I fell back...Back to the place I met you. I still follow your page and find great entertainment in seeing men struggle to find themselves in your inbox. One of them will succeed. I have no doubt. I'm just not that guy. I seek what I am. Authentic connection on all levels.

Such a connection doesn't require any games to played. Not even courtship is necessary. Connections are created in the stars to be experienced on earth. However, only conscious individuals have eyes to see them and the heart to grant them experience.

I digress...

August 21, 2020 - Kinda

The feeling was unique unto her. A very specific desire. A hunger. Not sexual but sensual.

He engaged all her senses. He inhaled her as he tasted her. Stripping her naked, he folded her in half and dove in... Face first. He was a slut for the fireworks of nectar that would erupt from her privacy. Nothing was off limits. She made herself available for the taking.

He mounted her. But he couldn't take her. She belonged to another man. Kinda.

Even in the height of passion he was rational and just. He knew that if he took her, she would feel guilty later. It wasn't worth it. She prided herself on being an honest woman. A woman of integrity. He wasn't willing to sacrifice her judgment for the pleasure of a sexual encounter. His discipline was an expression of love. So yes, the bed became a crime scene, but he made sure she could honestly look her man in the eye and say... "We never had sex."

August 22, 2020 - Square

He was a square. Naive. Unable to think outside the box. He came to me for advice about his love interest. He met a woman who possessed a strong spirit and found himself captivated by her charm. He explained that everything was fine until he confessed his feelings, then she became distant. I shook my head in understanding as he spoke.

He asked why.

I told him that he made a mistake by admitting his feelings. He wanted to argue about it, ranting about how it was rare for him to experience such strong feelings for a woman and he wanted her to know how she moved him.

"I get it bro. You wanted her to know that she was special."

"Exactly!"

I explained his mistake. He mentioned the "L word" and that turned her off. He didn't understand how. She was fresh from a divorce and wasn't looking for anything serious.

He was a harmless guy that she could enjoy spending time with but he was getting too involved. She associated love with commitment and commitment with pain. The pain she was trying to get past. He thought it was noble to spill his guts but it had the opposite effect. It didn't make her feel special. It made her feel trapped. She wasn't looking to be responsible for a man's feelings. She wasn't interested in the expectations that came with an emotional commitment.

"How do I fix it? What am I supposed to do?" He asked.

I encouraged him to treat her with a healthy dose of disregard. Give her space. He almost lost it. She had become an ever-present thought. He couldn't get his mind off her. The distance she placed between them was killing him.

"But my feelings are too strong. Why would I pretend they don't exist? That sounds like a sick mind game."

"Well buddy, if your feelings drove her off, your feelings are the problem. Fix your feelings and you might have a chance at the girl."

He rejected my advice and proceeded to send flowers to her job. Smh...

August 26, 2020 - Mono Gamos

The word monogamy stems from the Greek word monos (alone) gamos (marriage). Historically marriage is an economic institution. Thus, concepts like dowry and alimony come with it. In most polygamist cultures the husband can have as many wives as he can "afford".
It's all attached to economics. Government.

Some of us seek an unlegislated love. A love governed by spirit, not institution. Personal choice not obligation. A love based on absolute trust. Trust of character. Trust of individuality.

The woman who fears leaving her husband because she's financially trapped...is not a saint. She's not a martyr. She's not dying for a righteous cause. She's suffering at the hands of the institution. I'm not implying that marriage is a bad thing. Only 50% of them fail. It's a roll of the dice. What I'm saying is, a healthy relationship isn't strictly defined by the idea of monogamy. It's defined by the idea of "self-love". Once an individual has self-love, they can share it with anyone without the strings of institutional entanglement. Some of us want that. Some of us want what we are. There are different ways to love. None of them should be demonized. Monogamous love has a 50% success rate. Nothing that averages 50% can be upheld as the standard. But self-love is a 100%. I lean towards that.

That's all.

August 27, 2020 - Strength

She asked my opinion so I told her.

"I think you've been through a lot in life and you have grown to define yourself by your strength." She agreed.

I continued..."But your strength is like a weapon. If someone assaults you with a knife, you'll feel safer carrying a gun. You've been through a lot, so you carry your strength as a badge of honor."

"You feel safe. No one can harm you. You have a gun. Your strength. But life isn't about protection. Life isn't about defending yourself from harm. Life is about experiencing and evolving. Life is about the seed that rises from the soil and opens its pedals to the sun. It sounds beautiful but it's a scary process. It's hard to grow. Circumstances have taught us to seek security. We find security and think we are ok. But we are not. We are afraid. Why else does one seek security? Fear. Fear of being harmed, taken advantage of, used. So, we construct a life based around that fear. But that's not life. That's not living.'

"Life involves growing and expanding. Life exposes you to danger. The elements of life. So, yes, you are strong. But you are not living. That's your issue. You crave life but you have found safety. There is no life in safety. Only existence. You exist... but you aren't doing anything but being safe. So yes, you can celebrate your strength, but your strength is the source of your anguish."

August 31, 2020 - Eco Sexual

She said "If I had to describe my sexuality I'd lean towards poly, but I'd classify myself as Eco Sexual. I'm turned on by nature and natural things. Natural phenomena. Storm clouds that penetrate sunny days to create rainbows. That type of shit. I love it all."

She was a wild woman. Undomesticated, with an appreciation for male dominance. She explained "On a strictly sexual level, my primitive aspect is drawn to men who know how to pull hair. It's a huge turn off if men don't possess that quality."

She spoke about pheromones, chemistry, and the taste of forbidden flesh. She talked about power transfers and the exploration of her masculine energy. She didn't consider it kink. It was natural loving. The way she described fellatio would make a heterosexual man cringe.

She was so secure in her own sexuality that she demanded that in a partner. And since most men were sexually immature her desires lay dormant, patiently awaiting the universe to send her a host. She was beauty and the beast embodied as one. The main character of her dark fairy tale. She was the heartfelt pain that inspires classic love songs. A truth too powerful to deny, yet too powerful to embrace. Thus, her draw to nature.

Imagine a naked woman hugging a tree in the moonlight. Caressing the rugged bark as tender flesh. A woman who drinks rain, craves sunshine, and talks to plants. She was a one of one. A unicorn manifested as a modern woman. She described herself as Eco Sexual.

September 1, 2020 - Breaking

Breaking you is an act of love. If he really cares for you, he will break you.

You see...you are already broken. Your husband took care of that. He conditioned you a certain way. Now you are free of him but his conditioning still exists. You will carry that conditioning to the right man and he will be forced to break you...if he wants you.

You are like a broken bone that healed improperly. You must be broken, again, to correct it. He will be your surgeon and your opioid. He will pry you open exposing the unhealed fracture. He will break it, readjust it, and brace it in a cast. He will limit your movement for a while and be there to limit your pain. But he will be forced to break you...as an act of love.

September 1, 2020 - Good God

I wish that I wasn't so grounded in reality. It would make it much easier to love you or allow you to love me. But my heart is built different. My heart agrees with reality. And the reality is...

Life is about choices. People always have the right to change their minds. I wish that I wasn't ok with this. I wish I could muster up the strength to fight for you. But reality taught me not to fight for things. Reality taught me to "be" what I wanted. Reality taught me the virtue of selfishness.

If I have a need, I manifest it. Sometimes though prayer, meditation, hard work, other times through luck (favor). Either way, I'm immune to the idea of loss. People come. People go. That doesn't matter to me. What matters is the time I have with them. What I do with it.

Am I present, intuitive, conscious of my purpose in their lives? Do I create memories that inspire smiles? Does my presence remind them that God exists?

A great thinker once said, "To feel Good is to feel God."

So yes babe...you're gone...but I'm good.

September 3, 2020 - Inboxing

He saw me out with a beautiful woman and asked how we met. I told him Facebook. He asked me how. I was puzzled. "What do you mean? I just told you that I met her on Facebook."

He explained how he had been unsuccessful at meeting women on social media. Telling me sad stories of being left unacknowledged in countless inboxes. "They never respond!! It's frustrating!!"

He further confessed that he sent his latest flame four messages at the risk of appearing desperate. He had a really strong connection to her. She was very attractive and her posts resonated with his soul. He was enamored. Fascinated. But she ignored him.

"How did you get her to respond?" he asked. "Women like her have a thousand guys petitioning for their attention. They never respond to messages."

"Sir" I replied, "I understand your frustration but I don't share your assumption. I don't assume that women don't read messages. Yes, beautiful women are flooded with attention. Their inboxes are full. They have lots of fans on their pages. But that works to your favor. If a woman has an audience, it's because she likes attention. Private people don't entertain social media, so she's obviously receptive. Imagine her inbox. Say, 20 messages from random men. 5 dick pics, 10 “hey Beautiful’s”, and 5 guys writing paragraphs. Who has time to filter through all of that?"

"So, what do I do?"

"Be yourself."

"What does that mean?"

"Sir, right there, is your problem. If you don't have a self to be, she has nothing to acknowledge. Thus your dilemma."

September 5, 2020 - Trust

Trust is a delicate emotion that carries an abundance of magic. But if trust isn't tended... the magic will be lost.

She made the mistake of trusting him. But not really, because she was incapable of fully trusting anyone. Especially with her heart. She trusted him to be himself. Whatever that was.

And she secretly expected him to fuck up at some point. Trust made her uncomfortable. It exposed her to the possibility of getting hurt. But she really liked him, so she gave him a chance. All the while, expecting him to fail. That's what men do. According to her internal dialogue.

He succeeded in his conquest to covet her. She allowed him to. It was refreshing to be seduced. She was a guarded woman so she understood how to keep her distance.

But he was bold, persistent, and consistent. His antics made her smile. She liked him. More than she should. So when he fumbled the ball and broke trust, she pulled the plug on the relationship. Better to end it cold and sudden than to allow him to recover from his mistake. She had no business loving him in the first place. Love comes with trust.

If you can't fully trust, you can't fully love.

But even two halfhearted individuals can experience magic worth remembering. Memories worth holding on to. Seeing your reflection is a beautiful thing. It shows us who we are and where we are...emotionally. In the end we can only trust ourselves. Only then can we trust our reflection.

September 6, 2020 - Stubborn

Being stubborn is a tool I've used to sabotage good relationships.

I assume a "Take me as I am" posture and consciously push people away by being intentionally abrasive. It's childish and immature. Somewhere inside of me I don't feel worthy of love so I cling to "self-love" as a protection from feeling the possibility of abandonment.

I've been conditioned to think that everyone comes and goes. No one stays. So unconsciously I make myself inhospitable. I make myself a vacation...A get away.

But not a home. For you, I'm looking at myself through a different lens. A different light.

For you, I'm considering saying goodbye to my inner child and the tendencies that come with him. Rather than "Take me as I am." I'm considering "How can we grow?"

I'm wondering why that's such a frightening thought. Beneath it is the possibility of abandonment. If I invest myself in us, I lose my "I" to our "We."

For you, I'm wondering is that such a bad thing.

It's easy for me to spiritualize my fear of attachment. But today I'm speaking from my heart, not my spirituality. I'm speaking as a human, not a deity.

I'm thinking about giving you the power to hurt me in exchange for the possibility of becoming a better man.

September 13, 2020 - Breathe

I find myself being more like water than a tree. I have no position. I'm fluid. I move with the times. The vibe. I follow the flow. The current of life.

I've been playing tennis with the west coast for the past few years. Bouncing back and forth. I miss the west coast. When I lived in Hollywood I hung out with actors. When I lived in San Diego I hung out with hippies and yogis. When I came back to Dayton, I attracted everything I missed from San Diego. Out there a date is a hike. Everything is organic and the women love the earth.

Last night I reconnected with Hollywood. I hung out with actors. But no one was acting. Everyone was being real. Imagine a party of authentic individuals. Naked souls dancing and mingling. Celebrating freedom. Everyone was a celebrity.

The thing that stood out most...not one person looked at a cell phone. The moment was that rich. The current was that strong. The vibe was flowing and no one was blocking the flow.

I share this conversation because it reminded me of how precious fresh air is. If you live in a polluted environment, you can become immune to it. You only notice it was polluted by finally breathing fresh air. Somewhere on a mountain or in a rain forest.

I encourage you to climb the mountain to gain a broader range of vision.

I encourage you to take off your mask, remove your clothes, feel the rain... and breathe.

September 17, 2020 - Lights Out

She laid in the glow of a mind blowing orgasm. Catching her breathe, she looked to her lover and asked "How did you do that? My body has never done that before."

He held her closer and whispered, "I listened to you."

She said, "But I didn't say anything."

She was a woman who had lost touch with her voice. She had learned to put other people's needs before her own. In this regard, he was perfect for her. He was conscious. He paid attention to way she responded to his touch. She didn't have to say anything. Her body said it all.

She was the type of woman who only felt comfortable in the dark. She suffered body issues.

Her stomach was a source of shame. But, for him, it was a place of worship. A place where life originates. For this reason, he didn't enter her bedroom until she was mentally prepared.

She wanted him long ago but he declined her invitation. He understood that he had to deal with her in spirit before anything physical took place. She had an overactive mind and a highly guarded heart. It was a waste of energy to engage her mental. You couldn't convince her that she was perfect as she was. Her flaws occupied 80% of her mind state. So, he spoke to her in spirit. He left notes of affirmation in her pillow and in her underwear drawer. He spooned her in silence chanting words of power to her consciousness. He wrote her love letters so that she could see herself through his eyes while reciting his vision in her own voice.

He knew that she was ready when she removed her clothes without turning the lights off.

Lights out.

September 21, 2020 - Sorry

Saying "I'm sorry" is something I tend not to say. Sorry doesn't fit my vibe. To protect myself from saying it, I live a conscious life. I do things on purpose, with intention. Always aware of the cause and effect of my actions, I'd prefer to say I'm conscious than I'm sorry.

But hurting you made me realize that I slip up sometimes. I'm human. I hurt you because I have the tendency not to care about how someone feels about me. That was a mistake with you. So, thank you for checking me and reminding me that I can't treat you like the average woman. Thank you for reminding me to be more conscious. Your rejection has increased my awareness. The pain of missing you is a form of enlightenment. I realize that I have feelings...that I do care about how you feel. It doesn't feel good to miss you, which makes me aware of how good it feels to be with you.

So, I'm sorry. I'm sorry for giving more attention to my grind than to your heart. I allowed my selfish lifestyle to harm you. Selfishness has its limits. I'm learning that as I go. But true selfishness is when I acknowledge that we are One. You are a reflection of me. I see that now. Very clearly.

So, I apologize for the pain I caused you in order to learn this lesson.

September 22, 2020 - Playbook

I've learned that if a woman has a playbook, it's a trauma response. I recently lost someone I cared for because of this dynamic. We lost touch because the communication became toxic. She had this idea that I was supposed to text first each morning and initiate every phone call. If I didn't, she'd develop a silent attitude. We would finally talk and the natural flow would be off because her mind was hosting a quiet argument. She'd be thinking of why I was too busy to text, who I was with, etc. If I didn't text her she'd create a story of why. That story had nothing to do with the truth. It was her construct. She wrote a script based on pain from previous relationships. She couldn't comprehend that I'm old school.

Communication is very simple to me. If I give you my number I'll answer your call. Period. But she never called me because she didn't want to be a burden. She didn't want to seem "pressed for my attention". That's odd to me.

The result was the demise of our relationship because I didn't line up with her play book.

Again, I'm old school. I'd rather talk than text. I don't value texting as a valid form of communication. Yes, it serves its purpose if I'm running late or something like that. But it's not a valid form of communication. I'd never type out a paragraph with my thumbs when I can just push a button and have a conversation. Nor would I measure someone's texting pattern as evidence of their attraction, or lack thereof. That's silly.

Technology is a beautiful thing if used the right way. By "right" I mean honest. If you want to hear my voice...call. It's really that simple. That's honest. If you want to hear my voice (and wait for me to initiate the call) you're setting me up for failure.

In closing. Question your play book. It's a product of failed relationships that will ultimately recreate itself in your future.

September 22, 2020 - About Love

It was a sincere inquiry...

She asked him, "How can you claim to love someone and not care about losing them? If you love someone, you fight to keep them. You sound like a contradiction."

Not at all. It's an old prison habit called minding my business and staying in my lane. What's mine is mine. If something belongs to me, it can't be threatened so I don't fear losing it. And if I happen to lose something, or someone, they didn't belong to me in the first place. I'm ok with that. My love isn't based on holding on. My love isn't defined by possession.

The highest quality relationships in my life were designed by God. I trust Him to manage all of that stuff. I just mind my business and stay in my lane.

September 23, 2020 - Automatic

The connection, the energy, the vibe...was automatic. She took to him without conscious effort. He took to her with specific intention. She was the feminine energy that carried him through a long stay in prison. For years, he had searched for her physical manifestation.

And there she was...his unicorn. No longer an imaginary lover, but an actualized feminine presence ready to be loved. He loved her automatically. She loved him in return. He felt right. He fit. Which ultimately caused her to reevaluate her desires. She was committed to a man that wasn't committed to her. She had grown accustomed to being second in his life. Being faced with a someone who'd celebrate her as first, somehow, made her uncomfortable. She didn't know why.

After examination she found that she was comfortable being second.

She couldn't explain why.

So, the automatic connection automatically disappeared. Only to exist in a different time.

She was comfortable as a seed in soil. He was sunlight agitating her roots. Encouraging her to break soil and make herself seen. But she wasn't ready for center stage. Safer to be a backup.

September 23, 2020 - Him

God created him to feel things deeply. Both joy and suffering. But he was drawn to suffering.

His core belief was that light and love could heal any internal pain. He believed that if you poured awareness on a situation, you'd see it clearly. And from clear vision comes righteous moves.

He understood suffering. He had suffered a life sentence in prison. A decorated veteran of struggle, he was drawn to beautiful women with complicated souls. Those were his people.

Each relationship offered a unique opportunity to inspire healing. He could never belong to a woman because he already belonged to God. Thus, he was prone to follow his spirit, not a relationship. That was his blessing and his curse. He was incapable of turning his love off.

You could feel it in his eyes, his conversation, his touch. He possessed the power to make you feel seen. It was a gift. A spiritual tool of healing. If you can't see it, you can't change it. He represented light, and with his light came love. His love would make you receptive. His light would liberate you from darkness.

September 24, 2020

It was the same ole city. The city she was raised in. But she never truly saw it until she witnessed it through his eyes. A different lens. He was addicted to gratitude. He consciously searched for moments to thank God. His celebration of life stemmed from a childhood of incarceration.

His lifestyle was magical. He had the ability to challenge depression by counting blessings. His arsenal was composed of ten "I AM's" for every time life told him no.

She found herself in awe of his character, his perception, his story. His ability to fully absorb life and transform it into poems.

The gift of gab... He had it. Talking shit was an art. And if he chose to paint you with words, you'd feel them in private places. It didn't matter that his conversation wasn't exclusive.

It didn't matter that he talked that way to everyone. He had the power to ground you in the moment. And in the moment, he directed her attention to a visual worth capturing as a memory. The skyline... he saw the city and she saw the moon.

It was no longer the same ole city... It was a new city.

Life looks different in the presence of love.

September 26, 2020 - Devilish

She was being devilishly feminine. Knowing that he had a woman at home, she consciously chose to spend time with him. It was just one of those things. A friendship based on mutual curiosity. A pleasantly blurred line with sexual undertones.

One day she decided to test the boundaries.

Betraying their discretion, she intentionally scent-marked him and sent him home to announce her presence as mistress. "Why not?" She thought to herself, (giving the devil permission to stir up a situation.) "He says that she knows about me. He says they don't have secrets."

She chose to test the theory. He was oblivious of her ill intentions. He returned to his wife without a second thought. Wifey instantly recognized the new scent and complimented the mistress's taste in perfume. "Babe, call her and ask her the name of that scent. I need that in my life!" They shared a good laugh. She always liked the things that he liked...even his taste in women.

Moral: Openness and Honesty equal a "cheat proof" relationship.

September 27, 2020 - Tender

He brought his calmness to her storm. She lived a life of organized chaos. How she handled it was a mystery. But she did. He was a pause button for her drama. In his presence she could only feel peace and pleasure. He didn't believe in anything else.

She had been conditioned to manage the precarious emotions of a volatile husband. You never knew what would trigger him so she gave extra effort to create a life without disturbance for him. For her. For the kids.

The divorce was almost final. She went from being a suburban soccer mom to an inner-city hippie. She lived a life of simplicity and exploration. She roamed the city alone. She travelled social media as a free spirit searching for vibes. She found them. Too many of them. She became a safe box for people's darkness. Everyone felt comfortable confessing to her. Somehow, they sensed that she could make sense of their situations. The energy she once used to tend her husband transformed into tending the world. She was a "tender", because she was a tender soul which is why his presence meant so much to her. He effortlessly made her stand still and be present to the moment. He stopped time.

For once she didn't have to think. She had no responsibilities. All she had to do was be present. Her smile was his focus. Their conversations were great but their silence was greater. In their silence she could talk to herself about the joy he brought her. The joy of being free. The private joy of being present, alive, and tended.

September 28, 2020 - Contradiction

She was a sexual contradiction. Her body was perfectly thick. Made for handling. Her pussy was virgin. Too tight to be handled like her body.

He wrestled her into position. She loved how he bit her neck, pulled her hair, and took command of her presence. As he entered her, he understood the contradiction. Aggressive stimulation turned her on, but her privacy required more intimacy than force.

He took his time. Rather than fucking her, he focused on "feeling" her. He relaxed his urge to be inside of her and enjoyed the process of being with her. He nudged her clitoris with the tip of his erection until her body welcomed him with moisture. Her pussy was a lotus flower. It only opened to sunlight. He directed his light energy to his erection and gently stroked her outer lips with slow, probing, strokes. She opened. She clinched. She moaned.

Encouraging him to probe deeper. He listened to her body. He gave himself to her in conscious doses. It was their first time. She was mentally prepared to be disappointed. Most men had let her down. It was all about them. But with him, it was all about her. Not just in a sexual way. He connected to her deepest desires and her spiritual wishes. His touch communicated his love. His tenderness communicated his affection.

He revered her as a gift, a present. He opened her body to be present with her soul.

For this, she loved him in silence. Hoping he understood her speechlessness.

September 28, 2020 - Messy

A friend of mine started dating a woman I once loved. I was happy for him. He's a good dude. She's a good woman. They are a good fit for each other. A mutual friend asked me if I told him that I had once dated her. I said no. He seemed confused.

I explained that only a man who lacks character would do such a thing. My relationship with her is irrelevant to the state of her current situation. Revealing my relation to her would be a messy move. It would imply that I still had feelings for her. It would compromise their relationship. Who does that? I'm genuinely happy for her. I'm genuinely happy for him. Happiness is the result for everyone involved.

He mentioned something about keeping it real with him. Who cares to keep it real if the reality would end up in destruction. That's messy. I don't do mess.

Not all truths need to be told. And if truth is told it should be for the betterment of the person involved. Truth should never be used as a weapon to stir confusion and division.

What the fuck is wrong with people?

September 28, 2020 - Rolls

It was their first sleep over. They woke up in the morning from a sound night of sleep and he greeted her good morning. She replied, but something in her reply sounded off. He asked if she was ok. She attempted to duck the conversation so he probed deeper. He questioned the energy behind her hesitation and she reluctantly opened up. "I'm fine. I just figured that there would be...more. Afterall, I invited you to my bedroom."

He smiled and responded. "Sex... You were expecting to have sex?"

"Well yeah, kinda.. you know. You make me feel as is if something is wrong with me." He replied, "Babe, you're not ready to have sex with me."

"What do you mean? It doesn't get more obvious." she said.

He lifted her from the bed and stood her before her full-length mirror. Opening the curtains of her bedroom he exposed her image to the glaring sunrise. He removed her night gown and she cringed in her nakedness. He stood behind her and witnessed her discomfort through the mirror. She instinctively began wrapping her arms around herself for cover. She felt uncomfortable being naked. She had issues with her body. He wrapped his arms around her waist and began caressing her rolls. She squirmed in discomfort.

He turned her from the mirror, looked in her eyes, and reassured her, "This is why you're not ready to have sex with me. I will love on every part of your body. Parts that you don't like. Parts that bring you shame. Your personal discomfort will extend itself to my affection and that will compromise our connection. There is absolutely nothing wrong with you, on my end. But you perceive that something is wrong with yourself, so our connection can't be made."

"Does this make sense?"

It did, but it didn't.

Moral: Rolls are made for buttering. Muffin tops are made for nibbling. Some men clean the whole plate, thus if you aren't fully edible, you aren't fully accessible. You're not ready.

September 29, 2020 - Exploration

He explained to her that it wasn't about sex. She was experiencing anxiety at the thought of being alone with him again. She knew that she couldn't hold herself back. He reassured her that sex wasn't the objective. It was about exploration.

She had been married most of her life with lack luster sex. There was a fire inside of her that remained untouched. Desires unexplored. He fanned her fire and the heat travelled to her imagination. She visualized herself doing things that she had classified as taboo. He held her hand with understanding. Anxiety had become a part of her make up. Guilt shadowed her sexuality. Her body had changed after raising kids. Her husband only contributed to eradication of her self-esteem. She was lost inside of herself.

Feeling sexy was something that she had long since abandoned. All of her passion was directed towards raising her children. Now the kids were gone and she was forced to face her internal void.

He made her feel beautiful. It was an uncomfortable reality. But his attentiveness was so thorough that she had no choice but to believe him. He was a man who could have his pick of women, so for him to acknowledge her beauty casted doubt on her lack of confidence. The more she embraced the idea of being attractive, the more vulnerable she became. She eventually submitted to his vision of her. The anxiety disappeared. Replaced by excitement.

He drew a diagram of a naked woman and told her to circle the top three places she'd like to be touched. As she studied the image shame came over her. Only to give way to excitement.

He was encouraging her to use her voice and acknowledge her desires. The feeling was foreign but she went with it.

After completing her assignment, found herself naked with a fully opened mind. Unashamed and receptive. He took his time in taking care of her. Exploring her top three wishes he exposed her to more of herself. Subtle moans of approval turned into chants of yes.

"Yes!" turned into "Oh my god!" And there she lay...struggling to catch her breathe... Breathing for the first time in a long time. Glowing from the power of his intuitive attention. It was more than an orgasm. It was a coming out party.

October 8, 2020 - Untitled

The soundtrack for this picture is NWA, Spice 1, X-Clan, and Jodeci. I had never been locked up, and here I was with a murder case. It was here that I learned about the power of character and integrity. The value of having a good name.

Street Cred.

I entered the cell block and was greeted by someone from my hood. "Put your stuff up and I'll take you to the homies. I'll show you who to kick it with."

Turns out "the homies" were C.C. and Muff. They were my first introductions in the joint. I went to middle school with C.C. so there was history there.

I was naïve. I didn't know that prison had drugs and everything the streets had. I was blown away. But I learned quick. The homies had a lock on the market. They gave me the game. I learned how to smuggle drugs on visits. Eventually, I learned how to get an officer to do it for me. Character made these things possible. Trust.

Both C.C. and Muff served a lot of time only to come home and get murdered. So, I ask myself, what am I doing with my character and how can I prevent someone from losing a homie to the streets?

In closing, if you know someone who could benefit from my testimony, feel free to inbox me. Or if you know someone locked up and have questions about the experience. I'm opening myself to these conversations. Blessings.

October 10, 2020 - Starring

In film it's called the Leading Role. There's a reason why.

The Lead must possess the power to capture our imaginations. It must be a character worth paying attention to. Someone worth following and routing for.

Are you the Leading Role in your life?

I have to ask this publicly because I recently experienced a reality check. I joined a group of "like minds" and started sharing my writings. They became the source of controversy.

The women dissected my words for sexism. The men misunderstood my certainty as arrogance. When I stepped back to analyze what transpired, I realized that they weren't attacking me personally. They were responding to my position as the Leading Role.

Our life is our film. People who "lead" tend to be abrasive because most people follow. In society, the poor man gets sympathy. The rich man gets envy and hate.

If knowledge is power, confidence is wealth. When you write your own script and place yourself in the Leading Role people are bound to shun you. How dare you!!?

Again, I ask... Are you the Leading Role in your life?

Are you starring in your script?

October 10, 2020

She was a rare breed. The type to bend over backwards for people she loved. Effortlessly. God created her to embody creation. She breathed deeper than most women. She understood the essence of life. She had the power to put things in motion by standing still. There was great discipline in her posture. She stood tall.

When life produced a storm, she'd dance in the rain. When life seemed to collapse around her she'd fold herself in position to evade harm. Her flexibility to any situation in life made her "shero". Unstoppable. Seemingly protected by a force that even scholars didn't understand. Part empath. Part goddess. Which qualified her to lead, instruct, nurture. Her body was a teaching tool. Nature was her classroom. She possessed a force that inspired liberation. Rigid souls took notice of her. Fascinated by her will. Seduced by her willingness to submit. For in her submission was her power. In her power was a lesson for mankind.

She was a rare breed.

October 11, 2020 - Purpose Place

If I've ever led you on, or given you a moment so rich that you wanted it to last forever...I apologize.

I wish you understood where I come from. Serving life in prison will teach you how important the moment is. I take nothing for granted. I've been on a quest for freedom since I've been free. Outside of health...freedom is man's greatest value. I hold it dear. I enjoy sharing it with people. Your feelings are a product of my lifestyle. I showed you what freedom looks like...Feels like. For once, you could be your authentic self without judgment or shame.

For once, you could be a wild woman. Free to explore your sexuality. Free to embrace your desires. Free to challenge social norms and define a relationship on your terms, based on your most private needs. I don't blame you for wanting more.

You've been living life on the inhale. Inhaling everyone's stuff. Making sense of everyone's life. I provide you a space where you can finally exhale. I was placed in your life to introduce you to yourself. And now that you know who she is, you are empowered to honor her wishes. She has them. You know that now. I fulfilled my purpose. You have to fulfill your place.

October 11, 2020 - Loving Me

Have you ever looked in a stranger's eyes and saw something familiar?

Have you ever blessed a homeless man with a ten-dollar bill when he was only asking for spare change?

Have you ever felt moved to hug someone? Do you know the overwhelming craving to touch bodies?

Have you ever fallen in love with someone just because you showed up as an atmosphere of love? Do you know how it feels to break someone's heart because they were clinging to you and you were clinging to God?

Have you ever witnessed your private passion infect the people around you.?

Do random strangers trust you with their darkest secrets?

Do you live life with absolute certainty that God uses you to touch people?

Do you know the daily struggle of trying to manage a superpower, or balancing the erotism of your spirituality?

If not... please don't love me. I will hurt you. Rather, I will expose you to the fact that "you are hurting". It can't feel good to live in a cage. It can't feel good to live in fear. The freedom of my vibe will confuse your mind and aggravate your soul. Please don't love me.

October 11, 2020 - Solid

I had a dream that almost became a nightmare. We announced our relationship on Facebook and your inbox got flooded with messages from my past flames. They encouraged you to get out before it was too late. They sent mixed messages of how I was a good guy who was unable to commit to one woman. They attempted to offer you "friendly" advice. But somehow you saw through their intentions and politely told them "I know his character. I know his soul. One woman could never satisfy a man like him, because he craves a Queen. But thank you for the heads up. Please take time to heal. I pray that you find a happiness that exceeds your expectations."

It was the first time I fell in love inside a dream. Thank you for being solid…

October 13, 2020 - Story

The story you tell yourself about me is exactly that...your story. I have no investment in that. It's not my business. I'm in the business of being authentic. Transparent. It's better that way. It gives you the right to choose me consciously. I prefer that. There can be no misunderstandings when you deal in transparency. Yet misunderstandings occur because you'll ultimately take my vulnerability and form your own opinion of it, based on past experiences with men. I'm cool with that. I'm used to being misunderstood. I know that I'm not for everyone. But obviously we're vibing. So let's vibe.

Let's play with creation.

Do you know that life, as we know it, is nothing more than a series of vibrations? Do you know that energy as liquid and solids are illusions? Take into account that energy and matter can't be created nor destroyed. It's always been here in different forms. How cool is that?

We are blessed with a vibe, so let's create something special. We have the choice. Join me in the intention. Who cares how long it lasts? If life is always changing, let's change with it.

Let's not commit to each other.... Let's commit to having a good time with each moment we share. This is our story. Let's take fairy tales and create bedtime stories. We have the power to do so.

October 14, 2020 - Goldie

I have an angel named Goldie. I call her Goldie because she looks like sunshine and has a heart of gold. When I think of gold I think of "the gold standard". I think of how the US dollar used to be backed by gold. The paper dollar was only a symbol for the real thing.

Goldie is the real thing.

If gold itself is a precious metal, she's a precious human. As gold backs the dollar, she backs every value attached to her. She a rock. The rock of the family, and friendship. Everyone who knows her knows it.

Gold has nothing to prove. It's a God-given, sustainable, value by its very nature.

People with money are rich. People with gold are wealthy.

I pray that everyone has gold backing them. It's a hell of a feeling.

God backed Jesus. Jesus backs us. Golden people are God in physical form.

The world needs more gold. The world needs more God.

October 14, 2020 - Sacrifice

I disagree with you... I don't think that relationships are about sacrifices. I think relationships are about exchanging values. We all have good in us to give, and we all want to give it. That's one of the most fulfilling human experiences. Giving of oneself. Love.

Sacrifice is a dirty word. I don't want a relationship based on such a concept. I want a relationship based on overflow. Where my value increases your value and your value increases mine.

Sacrifice is an exchange for a lesser value. There is no balance in that. No harmony. No equality.

If love is a currency, I don't expect you to take a loss with me. I expect you to get a return on your investment. Losers chose "love experiences" that reinforces their sense of lack. The woman who cries about being used and the man who is the user, are the same person. They both operate from a sense of lack. Lack of self. Seeking to be defined and completed by the other.

That's not where I come from. I expect blessings. I consciously give myself to situations where I add value. Places where my overflow makes sense and benefits the recipient. That's the source of my spiritual favor. If you want a blessing, be a blessing.

As long as you attach love to the idea of sacrifice, your heart will continuously take L's. It's inevitable.

October 15, 2020 - Monsters Ball

He suddenly paused in the midst of foreplay. There was a series of fresh scars on her thighs. It looked as if she had fallen off a motorcycle or something. He felt a strange energy as he gently touched the abrasions. "What happened to you?" He asked.

"I happened..." She replied.

The gravity of her pointedness triggered his empathy. He felt a pain so intense that it was numbing. The desire to have sex was replaced by the need to connect and be fully present.

She grabbed his still hands and rubbed them on her body encouraging him to continue touching her. "Don't let that bother you. Keep going."

He pulled her into his arms and held her. She moaned and grinding into his body. He said "Baby, hold on. Let's talk."

"Fuck talking. Let's fuck. That's what you want. That's all men want."

He couldn't understand where she was coming from but he understood that she was coming from a place where he didn't belong. She had a history of sexual trauma that caused her to believe that men only wanted her for personal pleasure. The men of her past caused her to hate her body and demonize her sexuality. In the privacy of dark moments, she would cut herself with sharp objects and witness the blood trickle down her legs. It was a means of feeling alive. She had become so numb to life that only hints of death would awaken her senses.

She erupted into tears as he held her. A deep, weeping cry. "Please don't complicate this. Just make me feel good." she wept. He simply held her closer, in silence, and prayed over the demons that had possessed her soul. The monsters were balling.

October 16, 2020 - Grounding

He took her to a private part of the beach for a grounding ceremony. The sunset tossed vibrant colors across the landscape of the sky. The heavens rejoiced.

She pulled out her phone to take pictures as he embraced her from behind seeking to see what she saw, exactly how she saw it. He proceeded to blindfold her.

Darkness suddenly disrupted her photo shoot. She stood still, unsure of where this was going. It didn't really matter because she trusted him. The sudden lack of vision made her other senses awaken. She found herself being conscious of the sounds of the ocean and the feeling of the breeze on her skin.

He whispered on the nape of her neck while massaging her scalp. Occasionally grabbing handfuls of her hair. This symbolized his desire to stimulate the roots of her thoughts.

She gasped in pleasure.

He told her to feel the energy flow down her body as he followed the flow with his healing touch. He caressed her shoulders and wrapped his strong arms around her to massage her breasts. He rubbed her belly and pulled her hips closer to his body. He groped her thighs and knelt down to massage her legs. Burying her feet in the sand, he gave thanks for the earth and thanks for her presence.

"I love you." He whispered as he packed the sand snug around her ankles.

"I love you for surviving. I love you for every step you have taken forward and the steps that have taken you back. You are one with creation. So even though you can't see the sunset, I want you to visualize it through the blindfold. Can you see it baby?"

She nodded yes as the sunset and all the vibrant colors appeared from the darkness of her mind.

He stood to face her. She looked so vulnerable. So tender. He kissed her softly and told her that no matter if life blinds you to the beauty God gave you. It still exists even if you are prohibited from seeing it. Your vision comes from within.

Grounded.

October 17, 2020 - Untitled

It was a conversation with body language. He said, "Pose for me and tell me who you are."

She responded "I am goddess in the form of Queen. I release my breasts, free myself from society, and embrace my private comfort zone. I wear no mask. I need no face. The moon is my guardian. She has my back."

"I surround myself with clarity. Darkness hides stains. I adorn myself in white to emphasize my flawless presence. God doesn't make mistakes. My spirituality inspires creation. I'm beyond sexy. I'm sexual. Everything about me seeks to inspire...create. Without effort, I attract attention, which is why my privacy is sacred. So, I render you my back side. To have access to my face is to have access to my eyes. And to have access to my eyes is to have access to the windows of my soul. I can't give you that. But like the moon, in all of its transitions, if you have my back...you will have my soul."

October 19, 2020 - Knowing

It was a clash of spiritual values... Her intuition verses his knowledge. His knowledge was acquired through surviving the hood, the cell block, the city. Her intuition was a gift from God. This is where they differed.

His approach to life was based on hunting, gathering, and providing stability. Her approach was based on loving and feeling. She had everything she wanted except for the love she never had. This made her prone to his charm in a way she couldn't explain.

He wasn't just a man; he was a presence. His eyes and his voice made her soul sing opera. She instinctively knew who he was...to her. Somehow, she knew he belonged.

As she was motivated by love, he was motivated by creation. He would never sacrifice his passion to build for a love affair. Love didn't pay bills.

Slowly and painfully, she began to understand this. Swiftly and joyfully, she began to position herself as a value in his eyes. It was then that he began to notice her. Seeing her as she needed to be seen.

The shift occurred when she understood the power of knowledge. Rather than feeling what she felt and expecting him to feel the same way, she learned what he knew and empowered herself to speak his language.
In the Bible it reads "Adam 'knew' Eve, and gave birth to Cain."

Moral: If you want to create it...know it.

October 20, 2020

She had survived the darkness of life, which is why she was empowered to play with the shadows. If you threw her shade, she'd strike a pose. "Gratitude over attitude" was her anthem. She had learned the art of self-acceptance. Since she knew her truth, no one could tell her a lie about herself. She had evolved beyond valuing people's opinions to captivating their imaginations. She was a woman of fortitude.

She had a backbone. The phases of the moon were written down her spine, symbolizing the many dimensions of her divine femininity. Even her hips were lunar crescents, stirring the tides of deep emotion. Causing you to love her or hate her. But neither really mattered because she knew exactly who she was. Darkness had given her certainty...and certainty had given her light.

October 20, 2020 - Empath

The empath that cries about narcissism is like the Black person who cries about racism. Stfu and buss a move. Make yourself undeniable. I'm not wearing a mask that says, "I can't breathe." I'm not wearing a T-shirt that reads, "Black Lives Matter". I carry myself with power because I'm connected to God. Period. I'm no one's victim. I'm not asking for respect. I command it. I'm not asking to be liked or loved. My sense of self doesn't depend on public opinion. I know my history and my power. If a white person doesn't like me because I'm black...so what? And if I know that a system is in place that is not in my favor, my responsibility is to favor myself over that system. My ancestors laid the blueprint for my rise. I claim that.

Empaths are oppressed by the idea that they are victims. There are no victims, only volunteers. I see your ability to love as a superpower. You have the power to heal broken people. There is magic in that. But rather than celebrate your power, you parade your weakness. You were deceived, exploited, and disregarded by a person who lacks a conscience.

Welcome to Black America.

There is a silver lining. You can't use a person who has no value. The fact that you were exploited speaks to your value. Claim that and do something with it. Learn from your oppressor. If he can use you for his own self-interest, use yourself for your own benefit. There is great value in who you are.

I pray that you fall out of love with your suffering and in love with your power. I empathize.

October 21, 2020 - Low Key

The streets had taught him to keep his victories private. Success breeds envy. Better to stay low key. She petitioned him to announce their love on Facebook. He was against the idea. She took the liberty of upgrading her relationship status and changing her profile picture to "them".

He was a man worth having and she wanted to make it clear that he was off the market. She wanted to publicly celebrate their love, but her celebration became an advertisement. Women scanned her page, picked apart her flaws, and began plotting on her happiness.

"If that's what he likes, he's going to love all of this!"

They studied his personality and found common grounds of interest. It was a matter of time.

He was a man of character. An obvious advance would meet a polite decline. But most men have no defense when a woman is intentionally hunting for their affection.

Seduction is an intelligent, adult, sport. It's rare and can be refreshing.

Prior to changing her profile, women had only wondered what type of woman he liked. Her broadcast made him realizable...reachable...attainable. Simply because they judged her as a lesser woman, thus making them feel entitled to her blessing.

October 22, 2020 - Idea

Her life had been a series of ideas. The idea of being a proper little girl, a good wife, a responsible mother. Her life had been controlled by ideas.

Then she began to wonder where they came from. She began to question her master and unplug from the matrix. She was, literally, losing her mind. It was a beautiful thing.

Marriage taught her about incarceration. Divorce taught her about freedom.

Now she was free. So free, that she began to crave moments of belonging. She wasn't looking for love, or the "idea" of relationship. She just wanted someone to enhance her freedom and stimulate her sense of mindlessness. No ideas or expectations. Just pure presence and the intimacy that occurs when individuality is reflected.

He sensed her before he met her, and after meeting her, she accidentally kissed him goodbye with her tongue.

It was a Freudian Slip.

She found herself embarrassed. She found herself embraced. Afterall, she was free.

Free to be. Free to belong.

October 22, 2020 - Orange

She clenched the sheets and pulled them closer to her shivering body as he came up for air.

"My god!" She panted, "I can only imagine how many women you've been with to learn that skill."

"Not at all." he replied. "When I was a kid I used to cut oranges in half and pluck the seeds out with my tongue for recreation."

She never looked at oranges the same again.

October 22, 2020 - $40

It only took $40 and a bottle of wine to get her away. She was the type of woman who had grown accustomed to using the kids as an excuse not to get out. He gave her sister money to shop for baking supplies and asked her to make cupcakes with the children. He tossed in a bottle of wine as an added thanks.

When he called her, she was lounging in her depression. Sweatpants, T shirt, no make-up, hair in a ponytail. "I'm outside." She resorted to her usual spill about the kids as her sister knocked on the door.

No excuses...

He took her to the river with a tablet, bottle of wine, and a blanket. They talked.

He challenged her to write down the sources of her depression in a column. Five things came up. Next to the each of the five, he wrote two things that she could be thankful for. She looked at what he had written and began to cry. It was too much to accept that she was so blessed. Seeing it on paper gave it a different reality. It hit home.

She hugged him and cried, "Thank you." into his chest.

"We have an hour left. Come with me."

He took her to a cliff in time to catch the sunset. He removed his clothes and wrapped himself in the blanket. "Join me. Remove the fabric of your depression. Lounge clothes are your down clothes. Bring me your truth, shed your condition." She complied and snuggled into his warm embrace as the sun introduced the Eve, and evening introduced the moon. He narrated the scene and explained that life was about transitions. The coexistence of darkness and light. No need to deny your darkness but always celebrate your light. Agreed.

November 6, 2020 - Expression

She was a woman who loved to love. But love had taught her how 'not' to love because she had been betrayed by past lovers. There was a carefully constructed wall around her heart based on convictions that said, "I'll never let that happen again."

She didn't realize how thick the wall was until she found him. Her empathetic soul yearned to make life comfortable for him. The love she had been protecting suddenly had an outlet and she found herself revisiting old convictions.

Possessed by the desire to love him she slowly began releasing herself from the emotional bondage she had created. Her attachment to protection became a need for acknowledgment. She was like a wealthy person who lived in fear of being robbed. But no fear of robbery can exist with a person who is naturally a lover. She was naturally loving. She enjoyed making people happy. Meeting the needs of her loved ones.

In a moment of vulnerability, she opened her heart to him in a new way. A way that was spiritually refreshing. Her connection to him was undeniable. She could feel his pain and she took a chance to love him through his suffering. Transforming his pain into joy. Giving him the love that she was, and the love she so desperately wanted to receive.

It came naturally.

In the process, she saw that she had been resisting nature...her nature. Resistance became release. Release became acknowledgement and gratitude. He saw her for who she was. And in loving her, he gave her access to herself. She was truly love. But love is an action.

As thought becomes words, her love became a verb. Verbalized through expression.

November 8, 2020 - Love

Love me in a way that makes you feel fear. Then let that love transform fear into courage.

Love me in a way that makes you question your judgment. Then let that love transform your doubt into wisdom.

Love me in a way that would make people think you have lost your mind. For your mind is not needed.

Love me from intuition. Spiritual suspicion.

Love me from freedom, not caution. Love me from boldness not humility.

Love me selfishly, based solely on how I make you feel. Feel everything deeply. Even your anger.

Love me authentically. There is not a part of you that I can't handle. If you show me your inner bitch, I'll show her my inner magician. I will expose the illusion of anger as passion disguised. Then I'll show you how to channel that passion.

November 8, 2020 - Become

She was used to being fucked. Somewhere along the way she grew to appreciate the aggressive thrusts of a man inside her body. It became a staple of good sex. Part of it was the "people pleaser" in her. If the man was pleased, she was pleased. If she achieved orgasm, fine. If not, no biggie as long as her partner was happy. She wasn't used to intimacy and deep spiritual connection.

He was a man who approached her body for its inner truth, not its vanity. He approached her body as a vehicle of a spirit. Not as a fat ass and big breasts. As fabric adorns the body and becomes fashion, her skin adorned her spirit.

That's why he felt different. Her flesh was in the way. He removed it with his touch and entered her spirit. He tapped into her power and stimulated it. He blew on her flame and made her become fire. Every part of her being released moisture.

She sweated, she came, she cried.

Be. Come.

November 9, 2020 - Demonize

Their speculation that he was a narcissist wasn't totally unfounded. Life had taught him not to regard people's feelings. His only ethic was work ethic. He cared more about himself and his grind than anything else. Perhaps to a ruthless degree to the untrained eye. That's fair.

But life had also taught him Oneness. How he was energetically connected to other beings. Which is why he could move how he moved, without regard for your feelings, because he intended you to feel good. He didn't represent or reciprocate bad vibes. So what they perceived as narcissism, was really hedonism.

My question is, how did we come to demonize pleasure seekers. With all the sickness, hate, violence, and death in the world...how did we come to demonize someone who consciously seeks to feel good every, single second of the day. Even if it's at your expense. Who cares to live a life where you can't afford to show a person a good time, meet a need, or make a dream come true.

Y'all lost me there.

Nov 10, 2020 - Trade

She was in the darkest aspect of feminine frustration. Questioning herself. Questioning me.

"Why can't I find a good man that just wants to be loyal to one woman!!? Why is it so fucking hard!!?"

I inhaled the blunt and spoke to her bluntly. “You’re asking the wrong question. The question is... How long have you been chasing that illusion?"

She replied, "So you're saying no man can be loyal to one woman?"

"No. I'm simply asking a question. How long have you been chasing that illusion? You’re in your mid-forties. You haven't figured out how to love yet? Of course a man can be loyal to one woman because we can love different women in different ways. It's not sexual. It's not about monogamy. It's about trust. Love is synonymous with trust. Why can't you trust yourself enough to be ok with that?"

She said, "There you go flipping it back on me, like I'm being unrealistic about my expectations."

"Baby, you've lived this same reality for ten years. The love you are looking for has always evaded you. I'm not judging you. I'm making an observation. If your son repeated the tenth grade three years straight, you'd encourage him to get a trade. You've been at this for ten years to no avail. I'm simply suggesting that maybe you should learn a trade. We pursue higher learning to create a higher living. Perhaps a trade would allow you to create higher loving... Just a thought."

November 12, 2020 - Sex

When God is in your heart and magic inside your sexual practice you must be highly conscious of who you share it with. Everyone isn't ready for a transcendental experience, just as everyone isn't ready to be intoxicated by psychedelics. A recreational "trip" could become an experience of trauma.

An uninitiated soul can't handle the results of deep connection, just as a person with a closed mind can't handle the truth. It's overwhelming and will ultimately inspire rebellion.

Protect your spirituality.

Sex is a creative power. By nature, it serves two purposes. Creation of life. Creation of pleasure. However, pleasure is a subjective reality. Some people find pleasure in pain.

November 12, 2020 - The Moment

They were more than friends and less than partners. He sensed a shift in her energy and questioned her about it. Something had changed in her demeanor. She had introduced him to her circle of friends and they all embraced him. Some embraced him too much. She had no right to feel threatened but somehow, she did. Jealousy wasn't her thing, but something rubbed her the wrong way when women would advertise themselves to him. He didn't have to acknowledge their advances. The fact she saw it made her feel some kind of way.

She didn't realize that he was a reflection of her. A socialite. A magnet for broken souls. She had the unique power to make people question their convictions.
He was making her question her own.

She went into the relationship convinced that she didn't want anything clingy. Yet she found herself resisting the urge to hold on. He wasn't her man and she wasn't looking for one. But he was easy to be with. Nothing about him was uncomfortable. Her "go with the flow" approach was being challenged by a need she couldn't explain. A need to be something or someone...to him. Her feelings were getting involved.

She asked him, "What is your goal with me?"

He responded "Who needs a goal when we have the moment. The goal is to cherish the moment."

November 12, 2020 - Patiently

She loved him patiently through his evolution. He was a "take it or leave it" kind of guy and she took it like a champ. His highs, his lows. His warm embrace, his cold shoulder.

Loving him was, sometimes, a cold and lonely place. She suffered the pain of being isolated with her feelings. Her love didn't make sense. It wasn't something people were capable of understanding so she had no one to share her feelings with. Just him. But he didn't care about feelings. Which only increased her sense of loneliness.

Yet she loved him anyway. Intuitively knowing that she was supposed to.

Bound by a spiritual contract that committed her soul to his needs, even when he needed more than she could possibly offer. Her emotional conviction fueled her will to belong.

It took him years to realize a space within himself that could see her for who she was. And once he saw her, his resistance transformed into thanksgiving. Her love patiently witnessed him grow into her ideal.

November 13, 2020 - Creation

It was his creation... A relationship based on deep intimacy and emotional detachment.

How long could it possibly last?

He was trying to change for her. He gave effort to be a better listener. A better friend. He honored her wishes for more time, more this, more that. But the more he gave her the more she rejected him. Which wasn't really rejection, it was pause.

She couldn't trust his affection because he had conditioned her to remain distant. So his invitation to closeness couldn't be trusted. Her resistance to him was a reflection of his resistance to her. It was his creation...

In order to open the door to a higher relation, they both had to enter their keys into the lock at the same time. Hers into the dead bolt. His into the knob. The ritual of turning the keys at the same time would establish a new agreement and unlock a higher vibration.

But she paused...resisted...and it was her creation.

November 15, 2020 - Pushing

Pushing him away is not going to solve your problem. Anger and resentment aren't tools for healing. They will only give you more of what you don't want...Division. You want oneness.

Oneness comes from acceptance. If you accept who he is, your problem will be solved. Once you accept him...then you have a choice to embrace him or not. But loving him and pushing him away isn't productive. Your needs aren't being met by employing such a strategy.

Do you understand that force is used to resist or push away. You can't get your mind off a person you are trying to push away. The pushing, itself, requires all your attention.

I encourage you to try acceptance. Accept that he is who he is and then chose to deal with him or not. There is no force in that. There is no conflict. It's a choice to honor yourself and defend your peace of mind. The vegan doesn't resist eating meat. It's not a battle.

They simply choose to eat veggies.

November 18, 2020 - Love Life

"Love life" is like real life... No one knows when it will end. It's a shame to take it for granted. Better to be a selfish renegade. Live it while you have it. The beauty of the ghetto is like the beauty of prison. They teach you what's really important. Time.

What do we do with the precious time we have? I choose to love... Whoever I want, however I want. For the duration of a bar conversation or a long term flame. Doesn't matter. I'm showing up to show love. It's who I am.

My ability to love is what sustained me during incarceration. I have a relationship with my spirit. I trust my emotional judgment. I'm free to be a blessing. I'm free to expect blessings.

Love. Life.

November 18, 2020 - Running

She was running from herself and she didn't even know. She projected her private escape onto every man who expressed interest in her. She would strategically attract men only to distance herself from them. In her mind, men didn't really want her, they wanted something from her. She couldn't see that "she" was the prize. The collective body of who she was.

Based on her internal narrative she'd consciously set men up for failure. Constantly testing their loyalty. She got a thrill out of seeing men claw for her attention. And when a man would get close to her, feelings would develop, and she'd flee. Yet always looking back to see he was willing to chase her. In her mind, if he really cared, he would accept her challenge and prove himself. He would fight to be with her in spite of the obstacles she placed before him.

She asked me if she was wrong. I said "No, not at all."

"Then why do I keep doing the same thing over and over?"

"Because it works for you."

"No, it doesn't. I just want a guy to step up and be real."

"Sounds good, but based on your actions, apparently, it works for you. It gives you the advantage of being right. You pride yourself on your intelligence... your ability to anticipate a man's failure. When it manifests you celebrate your emotional IQ.

All along you are creating the experience of self-righteousness at the expense of being loved."

"I don't like you Sol..."

November 19, 2020 - Packaging

If she's used to getting the short end of the stick and you give her your all...she will reach for what's missing.

If she has daddy issues, and you enter love with her, those issues will become yours.

If she inherently believes that she's not enough, you will never be enough for her.

The challenge of loving such a woman isn't impossible. It just takes time, consistency, mantras, and angels. It requires cleverness and seduction.

Damaged goods are still edible. They can still be opened and prepared for consumption. The key is not to value the packaging over the content.

November 21, 2020 - Understanding

If you enter love with an understanding, no misunderstandings can occur. In the event they do, they are easily healed by the "understanding" that created the relationship.

In life...all things are selfish. Energy needs expression. God needs praise. A baby enters the world requiring your undivided attention. All things are selfish. Knowledge is power. The more you know, the more you can do.

Understanding is power. Once you have it, you want more of it because it provides security from danger. When you begin a relationship with understanding, that energy seeks to create more of itself. It seeks to expand. The broader the foundation the more opportunity there is to build.

Then it becomes a matter of sharing a vision. But again...all things are selfish. Two people can see the same thing differently. Which is why understanding is so vital in any healthy relationship.

November 23, 2020 - Pray

I pray that you encounter an undeniable connection. Trust, passion, and love, all at once.

I pray that he gives you 5-minute hugs and never tires of kissing you.

I pray that he grabs your ass while you do dishes and kisses your shoulder as you fold laundry.

I pray that you find someone worthy of taking a day off for. Playing hooky and day drinking.

Like the old days.

I pray that you find someone who ignites your youthful spirit. Someone to laugh with. Someone who requires no effort. Someone who's silence is as beautiful as his conversation.

And when you encounter him, I pray that you are courageous enough to hold space for him.

November 24, 2020 - First

She needed him to place her first.

He needed her to place herself first.

This was the source of their emotional conflict. She felt like he would potentially leave her for the next best thing. But if she knew that she was the best that she could be, none of those insecurities could exist within their bond. Instead, their relationship became toxic.

She became emotionally repressed. When she'd finally give voice to her emotions the voice would be loud. Her repressed anger would be expressed violently. She was hurting inside. Hurting even more because he was incapable of understanding her feelings. So even when she expressed them there would be no resolution.

She just wanted to be first. She wanted to be his all. But his private ambition exceeded the idea of a woman. His motivation surpassed the idea of being a husband. He was prone to follow his spirit.

What was he to do?

Kill his spiritual drive in order to honor her emotional needs?

Not likely. So he made a conscious choice to deceive her. He chose to love her with lies until she finally believed that she was enough...as she was.

November 24, 2020 - Savior

She came to the conclusion that he wasn't a player...he just suffered from a savior complex. His inner child was still trying to take care of his mom and deliver her from low-income housing. He found in women, pieces of his mother. Beautiful creatures trapped in a circumstance.

His instincts were more powerful than his judgment. He couldn't resist the urge to deliver you from ideas that held you hostage. The ghetto is an idea. Divorce is an idea.

She noticed that the women he loved were all similar. Some fractured. Some broken. All providing a void for him to fill. A space for him to stand out.

Surviving prison empowered him to teach freedom. The women in his life were trapped emotionally. Some suffered guilt from the past. Others suffered anxiety about the future. All needing grounding and remembrance. They needed to be reminded that they could stop time and change the narrative. His mom felt trapped financially. The women in his life felt trapped emotionally.

It was his divine duty to minister forgiveness and gratitude through sharing his emotional abundance.

He wasn't a player. He was a vehicle. And what good is a vehicle if it doesn't deliver you from point A to point B.

November 25, 2020 - Self Love

She knew he was a narcissist but she loved him anyway. He was good for her depression. He gave her a story to believe in. An opportunity to be special.

He had the power to take her away. Out of her head and into her spirit. Average men would eventually become a source of boredom. However, he held her interest. He knew how to go deep. She needed that.

He made her the center of the world. He reminded her that she was the source of the reality she was experiencing. He paraded selfishness as a virtue. Encouraging her to seek victory in all of her decisions. Seducing her into trusting her own judgment. He inspired her to face the guilt of putting herself first.

She knew he was a narcissist but she loved him anyway. He was a lesson of self-love.

November 25, 2020 - Gangsta

You must be Gangsta to love a Gangsta. Otherwise you will end up lost in the wilderness of your own deceptions and insecurities. When a beautiful woman chooses a celebrity, she already knows what it is. She knows that his lifestyle will expose him to women who she perceives as more beautiful, more fit, more this, more that. "Gangsta" is her ability to know herself and play her part in his life.

Gangsta is entering the relationship with understanding and trust. Gangsta is knowing that your role in his life is irreplaceable because you play it so well. If you aren't Gangsta, your choice in partners should remain within your emotional price range.

Gangstas approach life as a disciplined team sport. Trust is the glue that keeps it together and the fuel that makes it function. If you have no concept of team, stay away from G's. If you're looking for "happily ever after" find a husband and pray he doesn't cheat. But in the arena of Gangsta love there is no concept of cheating.

From the beginning you'll know that you are a part of a network of individuals who share the same vision. Everyone must play their part and trust the supporting cast. No ego can be involved. That's why the military breaks the soldier down before they build him up. They kill his ego. Ego will cause internal war within the unit. If the lieutenant wants to be the captain and the captain wants to be the general, there is dysfunction in the ranks and nothing can get done.

Bottom line... "If you don't understand the concept of team...stay away from G's".

November 27, 2020 - Chillin'

Her loyalty and common sense were constantly at odds. It was a war that she didn't choose. It was given to her by years of failed romances. Years of staying too long, ignoring the signs, and suffering disappointments. Again and again.

Her past was the background for his shine. He wasn't someone she could take seriously, so the possibility of being hurt didn't exist with him. And regardless of what he did in her absence he always seemed to make time for her. He showed up when she needed him most.

Not often... Just the times when she was tired of the dating scene and wanted to be in good company.

With him, the war didn't exist. He provided a cease-fire to her consciousness.

With him, she could exercise her loyalty and common sense without fear of disappointment.

He was cool... And with coolness comes the ability to chill.

Ask her what she's doing..."Chillin'"

November 27, 2020

There are some women in the world who possess the "it factor"...

I've known petite women who had psycho-emotional issues. I've known small women with eating disorders. Their obsession was to remain thin. It was a constant, ever present, demon.

It governed how much alcohol they drank and how many calories they consumed with each meal. I've known thin women who wanted to gain weight but couldn't.

There is something to be said of the full-figured woman who claims her body type. The woman who embraces the fact she's not meant to be thin.

Living in Hollywood taught me a lot about vanity. Living in San Diego taught me a lot about "being". The west coast is holistic and filled with beaches. Which means a lot of women eat right and spend time in bathing suits.

Imagine the audacity of this woman.

With self-realization comes boldness. With boldness comes respect and admiration. .Her full-figured presence made small women question why they weren't ok with themselves.

Quintessentially thick.... even Barbie looked at her and said "Damn!"

November 28, 2020

She was a strong black woman who had been seduced by the power of the patriarchy. So strong that her demeanor became slightly masculine. She was also a vixen. Men were drawn to her in a primal way. She used this to her advantage. Molding men to serve her will. She was a skilled teacher of men. Each time she conquered a man she felt the orgasmic sensation of ego gratification. She psychologically experienced victory over the men who had taken advantage of her as a young girl. She had to be tough to overcome her childhood trauma.

That toughness became a way of life. Even her love was tainted by the fear of being a victim.

She practiced tough love. She loved with the passion of a lion tamer. Submission to her will, would get you a treat. She knew how to teach men.

She weaponized her sexuality. It was the one aspect of her being that was undeniable. The one thing that could control men. Even if she dressed down and wore no make-up men still noticed her. It was an inevitable occurrence in her reality. She learned how to manipulate her magnetism. In doing so, she lost her taste for love and replaced it with a thirst for power.

November 28, 2020 - Mathematics

She said "With you, sex is always on the table. You use the term 'friend' very loosely."

This was the foundation for her distrust. I spoke to her in terms of vibes and auras.

Women who love yoga carry a certain vibe. People who love God radiate a certain vibe.

Thus is true for a man who has self-love. I agree, with me, sex is always on the table because I am sexual. I care about feeling good and creating things. But for me, sex isn't about the physical connection, it's about the energetic. I like being around people who make me feel good. I enjoy making people feel good. It has nothing to do with wanting to sleep with women. It's about stimulating thought and enhancing the creative force.

She continued... "Plus, you don't have many male friends. All of your friends are women."

I explained to her that I spent 18 years locked up with men. I'm over it. Men have the tendency to compete. Women want to connect. So being around feminine energy offers me the best opportunity to create. Two dicks can only create friction. Add the feminine to the equation and the friction creates magic. It's mathematics.

November 29, 2020 - #Only Fans

It only required the acknowledgment of a vibe and a few texts, and she began to open up. Realness and transparency held them in common. She confessed "Don't judge me but I'm a sex worker."

His response was both surprising and stimulating. He responded "I applaud any woman who takes command of her sexuality and uses it to her benefit. To me, she's a modern-day queen. What other woman is self-governed in today's society? Being successful is not the same as being self-governed."

Many women go to college and acquire huge debt to make themselves attractive to the job market. The ones who get chosen become successful. But the acquisition of a degree doesn't guarantee a lucrative job. How powerful is it for a woman to use herself as the primary resource for her success? That's a queen. A self-governed woman who relies on herself to make her way. She sits on a throne and controls the traffic of her life.

A "stay at home wife" is subject to her husband's judgment around finances. She's a slave.

The dual income household is better, but both parents are absent for most of the day and tired when they get home. An independent woman works her ass off to provide.

But a queen has the power to make a month's income in a single day and have her time for her kids and whatever recreation she chooses for herself. She's far more peaceful because she doesn't live to grind. She grinds to live. She has her way. Not too many women can say that. Not too many women are queens."

November 29, 2020 - Passcode

He noticed that her head would shift every time he grabbed his phone. She was eyeing his passcode. He was very careful in concealing it.

One day he "accidentally" allowed her to see it while they were drinking having a good time. He made a run to the store and purposely left his phone home. He returned and the mood had changed. The good time was over. She was pissed. Crushed. Yet still pretending that everything was ok.

He wasn't her man. He was a man to her, not for her. But she hoped he'd one day be hers.

What she saw in his inbox blew her away. She scrolled his text messages and became devastated. Every woman who corresponded with him was better than her. In some way. More fit. More attractive. More stable.

She silently began to ponder why he was even with her.

She didn't understand that she was beautiful. Her idea of beauty was something other than herself. That was her essential flaw. She lacked self-knowledge, thus her self-worth was compromised

He asked her "What's going on babe? You seem distant."

"I'm good. Just tired."

He understood. She was tired of thinking about the wrong shit.

Moral: Seek and ye shall find. And what you find could ruin a good time.

December 1, 2020 - Mess

She said "He married her and wasn't going to tell me. I had to find out on my own. But he keeps coming over here. If he's so happy with her, why would he keep coming back here?"

Perhaps because women can serve different purposes. The wife is someone you build with. Perhaps you're just someone he sleeps with. No judgment. It's just a reality. Men can hold different spaces and positions for women. Love is a dresser that has different drawers. Each hold specific items.

Apparently, what he created with you was specific unto you. Obviously, it works because you still welcome him to your bedroom despite his choice to marry someone else.

Either you're dick whipped or a messy optimist. If it's just about the sex, keep it about the sex. Nothing wrong with that. But if you take issue with him choosing another woman, well...

That's just messy.

One would argue that the whole scenario is messy. I disagree because I find beauty in consensual adults making choices that support their self-interest. But you can't be the sock drawer seeking to be the walk-in closet. That's mess.

December 1, 2020

She wasn't embarrassed or ashamed. She was beyond humble. She didn't want her face to be seen because she didn't want the credit for her accomplishments. She understood herself as a vehicle. She was a teacher. Her pride stemmed from raising students to teachers.

That's all.

But the world was fascinated by her teachings. They were fascinated by what she could do and how she could do it. She was a body builder and a body healer. She used the physical form to communicate a message. A simple message. "You can do anything that you put your mind to."

So disbelievers saw redemption in her pose. And believers saw grace. Either way, she won your perception. That's all she needed to fulfill her calling. But she didn't want the credit. She didn't want the praise. She only wanted to be...

To serve and exemplify. She was faceless, but you still saw, exactly, who she was.

She was the power of humility.

She wasn't embarrassed or ashamed.

December 2, 2020 - Male Empath

We often hear stories of the female empath who suffers at the hand of the male narcissist. But what about when the roles are reversed? I'm not a fan of the modern labels to describe the dynamic. Narcissism has become trendy. Too me, the empath is simply a lover and the narcissist is the unloved. That's the story line.

So what about the man who loves a woman who is unloved. The man who sees a potential in her that she doesn't see in herself and foolishly tries to love her into it. Only to create a toxic circle of emotional failures. Suffering the spiritual anguish of not being enough yet still giving more to fulfill the promise of his heart. Only to meet deeper levels of rejection.

What about him?

My comrade recently gave up on his beloved, because she was unloved. There was nothing he could do to fulfill her. There was nothing he could do to make her happy. He became a better listener, a better partner, a better friend, only to realize that he was powerless to change her.

So he gave up. Not with anger or a sense of defeat. She had beat him down emotionally until he realized that he was giving his love to the wrong person.

She was possessed by a fear of abandonment and would unconsciously push him away to validate being afraid. The more he gave, the more she rejected. She lived from a narrative that said, "All men leave." So he left. Proving her right.

Even in his leaving he was giving... Giving her exactly what she wanted.

December 4, 2020

The shadows made her interesting. They gave character to her presence.

She was a student of vulnerability, empowered to be naked and unafraid. A nocturnal soul...she understood the shadows. The shadows evolved her humanity. More than woman. A virago.

A woman who possesses masculine strength yet exalts her femininity. A female warrior.

Misunderstood by people who lacked duality. People who thought things had to be only one way.

Advocates of darkness. Advocates of light. Then there was her...

Gracefully sitting in the shadows. Teaching both sides, there are more ways than one.

December 5, 2020 - Floorplan

Her hostility towards him stemmed from an illusion. She was expecting him to be other than himself. And all he wanted was to be the best version of who he was. His personal ambition was to expand his individuality and manifest his highest potential. He was blinded by positive, creative, vibes. When she became negative, he would lose sight of her. This would only increase her negativity because she felt ignored...dismissed.

His effort was to protect "peace of mind" at all costs. Even at the expense of their relationship. She was becoming an emotional migraine. A thief of solace.

He had to walk away. He wasn't a fan of domestic violence in any form. There were too many women in the world who felt good to entertain the bad.

Conflict and misunderstanding aren't building tools; thus she lost her place in his floor plan.

He was designing a house built on pleasure and love. Each room serving as a sanctuary.

The space she once held was part bedroom, art studio, and man cave. He would go to her to decompress, sleep, create art and make love.

But she wasn't happy with the floor plan. She wanted to be the only room in the house, which would have made the house a barn.

December 6, 2020

It was an artistic mating call between a poet and a muse. He petitioned her to tell a story with her body and allow him to share that story with the world. She danced into his imagination, stirred his spirit, and posed for his study.

He began to speak...

"She placed her higher self in the seat of her lower self and raised her lower self to the sky.

Exposing her rose petals to the sunrays, witnessing herself procreate with the light.

A lunar delight. The illusion of night. Proof that moonshine is, in fact, sunshine.

She defined...paradox. She personified understanding. Her world seemed upside down but she was just under...standing."

December 10, 2020 - Pushing

Pushing him away is not going to solve your problem. Anger and resentment aren't tools for healing. They will only give you more of what you don't want...Division. You want oneness.

Oneness comes from acceptance. If you accept who he is, your problem will be solved. Once you accept him...then you have a choice to embrace him or not. But loving him and pushing him away isn't productive. Your needs aren't being met by employing such a strategy.

Do you understand that force is used to resist or push away. You can't get your mind off a person you are trying to push away. The pushing, itself, requires all your attention.

I encourage you to try acceptance. Accept that he is who he is and then chose to deal with him or not. There is no force in that. There is no conflict. It's a choice to honor yourself and defend your peace of mind. The true vegan doesn't resist eating meat. It's not a battle. They simply choose to eat veggies.

December 10, 2020

He had become a fan. Liking and loving her posts. She was used to assessing male attention and analyzing intention. She saw something in him worth protecting so she responded to his advances.

She said "I appreciate your compliments but your interest in me would change your life in the wrong way. I know that you perceive me as exotic. I know that my image stimulates your lower self. That's why I'm responding to your message. My message to you is to protect your marriage or end it. Your interest in me is purely sexual. I'm not put off by it. I'm just aware that if I entertain you, I'll end you. An experience with me would alter the stability you've created for your family. An experience with me would change you forever. Do you know why vampire movies are so captivating? Do you know why the bite of a vampire symbolizes a transformation. From mortality to eternity? No. That's why I politely decline your attraction. I'd end you. I'd make you a different person. That would not be fair to your wife or my spirituality."

So like me from a distance. Appreciate my presence as an observer, because if you participate in who I am you will lose yourself and everything you know to be normal. I'll take you so deep into your darkness that you'll lose a taste for light... Are you ready for that? Yes, but no. I know your answer because I know your spirit. Remain a fan, because if you become a friend...it won't be friendly."

Nothing else needed to be said.

December 12, 2020 - Messenger

I didn't know his wife was following me. She hadn't liked or shared any of my work so I didn't take notice of her. But privately she had been sharing it with her friends. I had become a part of her conversation. And apparently, I had thrown a few likes her way. So, he inboxed me and asked me why? (Disclaimer: I can be an asshole.)

So I played along. Just to see where the conversation would go.

"Sir" I politely responded... "Are you under the impression that you are the only man who likes your wife?"

The bubble appeared. He was typing. Then it disappeared.

It came again. He was typing...Then it disappeared again.

This went on for two whole minutes. Literally.

GTFOH

December 13, 2020 - Surface

On the surface, everything was perfect. She made it that way. It was her job. She was obligated to protect the image. Even though she ate shit every night.

To uphold the image...she had to eat shit.

On the surface, everything was perfect. But inside she was dying. Intuitive men would notice her suffering and ask her if she was ok. Her automatic smile would appear and politely shun their inquiry. It was her secret. She had to protect it, along with her illusion of a perfect marriage.

On the surface, everything was fine because the kids were in a safe environment.

But it wasn't really so safe. In fact, it was a crime scene. The kids were witnessing their mother get murdered at the hands of their father. But dad seemed innocent because she never said shit. She never complained. So when he demonized her, she had no defense. His narrative prevailed over her silence. He painted her as a bitch while she was pretending to be the perfect wife. It worked. He turned everyone against her. Successfully isolating her to serve his will.

However, his success was his failure. For in killing her... he was killing himself.

But they were monogamous.

December 22, 2020 - Toxic Spirituality

I've been seeing the term Toxic Spirituality lately. I haven't taken time to research it because I like to use common sense and deductive reasoning. I like to simplify.

I instantly thought about the dualities of life. There are negative and positive spirits.

Then, I imagine the people who create sophisticated counseling programs based on catchy themes.

Toxic Spirituality.

Where does this term come from? Priests have been exploiting lil boys for centuries and charismatic preachers have been pimping people for years...

Where was this term? Now it seems to be a trendy concept. Labels come with division and judgment. The negative and positive coexist. So what? Humans can be angry or happy, demons or angels. So what?

Labels and catchy themes don't bring healing. They don't even bring awareness. They only bring division. With division comes fear, which is why divide and conquer is a real war principle.

Stop being so spooky people.

December 22, 2020

The beauty of her sadness was found in a moment of despair. She was done with life...but still living.

There is nothing like the awareness that hits you when facing death. Life flashes before your eyes. She saw her collective experience stream through her awareness. A download of suffering.

There was nothing to hold on to. Even her physical beauty was depressing. She was so attractive that people assumed she didn't have problems. Which only made her more lonely in her darkness. Knowledge is light. Knowledge...to know your ledge.

She was on the brink of giving up. There was no way out. No reason to keep going. No one could talk her off the ledge. No one could save her. In truth, she didn't need saving.

She only needed a dark moment with herself and the idea of death...the idea of giving up. It was in this moment where she saw a light she couldn't explain. A light that held her even when she wanted to let go.

The beauty of her sadness was found in a moment of despair. She was done with life but still living. This simple awareness made her alive in a way that made her realize she was stronger than her depression. Yes, there was still something to hold on to. But it was within, not without.

December 23, 2020 - Spiritual Playboy

I don't take offence when I'm misunderstood. I've been accused of being all sorts of things. But recently I was labelled a "spiritual playboy" from someone who knows me personally. This term was introduced to her by a "spiritual" group she belongs to. I was tempted to take offence, but instead I took notice.

I noticed that the conscious community is not so conscious. In society, there is a sheep mentality in operation. That mentality is within the conscious community as well. Groups are formed for like-minds. I understand it. I just assumed that the conscious community was above limited thinking.

The spiritual playboy was contrasted against the king, as the narcissist with prince charming. Such comparisons disgust me. I'm an essentialist. Good and evil are at the essence of all human beings. A playboy is an extension of the ladies' man. The question becomes... Can a ladies' man be spiritual? Can a man love multiple women without it contradicting his spirituality? Of course, yet labels like this are established to identify a certain prototype of man. It seems that the mental health world is much like the healthcare field...they get paid to perpetuate disease. There is no profit in healing. Smh...

December 23, 2020

She told him a story about darkness... How it provides the background for stars to shine.

She described herself as "the morning star". Her understanding of the world was Luciferian. She told him how Lucifer was associated with Venus even though the figure was portrayed as a masculine entity historically. She traced her lineage back to the origins of Eve.
Once upon a time she was the rib that protected man's heart. She explained why men were emotionally vulnerable, and how easy it was to influence Adam to betray God.

She broke down the hierarchy within Gods kingdom. How Lucifer was the most celebrated angel, presiding over music and the arts. In her world, darkness was a friend and fear was a tool, not an emotion. She knew how to use fear to make you feel alive. Inspiring blood flow.
She concluded her story about darkness as dinner arrived.

She consciously cut into her steak and salivated as she witnessed the blood ooze from the tender filet. Dipping the fork into the blood she slowly raised the meat to her mouth and savored its tenderness. She closed her eyes, moaned softly, and chewed attentively.

The end... or perhaps the beginning. For darkness has no sense of time.

December 27, 2020 - Voiceless

There is a unique danger in loving a woman who has been oppressed by marriage. A woman who was denied a voice. Once she finds herself enough to claim her voice she becomes a threat. Like a teenager who gets bullied and retrieves a gun. Too much power, not enough experience.

The woman who has been oppressed and finds the power of her voice is a special kind of creature. She might hurt you by accident. Her voice is a pistol and she is no longer afraid of the bully. Dangerous. She's subject to cut you with words. It's an involuntary response to her trauma. She had bitten her tongue for so many years that speaking became a superpower. A blessing and a curse. Sometimes she'll say things just to know that she can. Just to exercise her right to speak. It's more about her than it is you, so don't take it personal.

Give her room to speak. Allow her to shoot. Understand that she has a hair trigger and stay out of harm's way. But if you happen to get shot, don't panic. Know that she didn't mean it, even if it hurt. The military calls it friendly fire.

December 27, 2020 - Resistance

She invited him to resist her. He accepted her invitation and overcame her resistance.

Even in her submission she was resisting. Resistance was an unconscious urge. To the point, she would fight against nothing. She couldn't even kiss without fighting. She loved his oral attentiveness and hated herself for loving it.

Red flags weren't enough. She needed more reasons not to like him. None were found. In fact, she found the opposite and opposed herself for finding it.

"You're toxic AF." He laughed.

"If I'm so toxic, why do you deal with me?"

"The same reason doctors deal with patients."

"So, you're going to heal me?"

"Nope. I'm simply going to show you that there is nothing to fear. If there's nothing to fear, there's nothing to fight."

That's all.

December 28, 2020 - Damn

It was a casual meet and greet. A simple conversation over a margarita. It went well. So well, that it ended with a kiss. A kiss that caused her to crave other forms of intimacy.

Over time he warned her. "It's obvious that we have great chemistry but it's important for me to let you know that the idea of love is off limits."

She asked why.

He explained "Your idea of love is based on pain experiences. You associate the idea of love with pain. Every love you have experienced lead to pain. So let us never go there. You will unconsciously drive our love into pain. It's inevitable."

She imagined that he was trying to practice reverse psychology on her so she challenged his boundary. "I disagree. What if it worked out? How can you be so sure it won't?"

He explained. "The very idea of it working out means that pain will be the result. Every time love has been involved with you so has pain. You don't have a reference for the type of love I'm capable of giving. For me, love is a freedom sport. Catch and release. Loving everyone that comes into your life without the need to capture them. For you, love is hunting to kill. And I don't want to die."

Damn...

December 30, 2020 - Gas Lighting

Funny story.

In San Diego I was staying in a high rise downtown in an area called Gas Lamp. At the time, I was hanging out with a woman who accused me of "gas lighting" her. It was the first time I ever heard the term. I thought it was something unique to the area - like mannerisms or a way of speaking.

I clarified "You mean Gas Lamping?" She said "No. Gas lighting! You always try to make me feel like I'm imagining things."

In truth, she was... She was imagining a relationship with me.

We discussed boundaries. She held my arm at the bar as if she was my woman. I expressed my discomfort with her display of affection. She tried to make a statement to the other women at the bar, making it seem as if we were a pair. It was all a product of her imagination. I simply checked her on it.

I wasn't gas lighting... I was clarifying the flame.

December 30, 2020

My pen was seeking inspiration, and it bumped into her. I couldn't tell if she was a model or just modeling. Perhaps it was just a fun photo shoot. I introduced myself and asked to use her picture for a post.

"Which one?" she asked.

She wasn't happy with my selection. I can understand why because there were so many powerful pictures that I could've chosen from. I saw them. They were dope. Some sexy. Some profound. But this one spoke to me. It came across as a moment of upstaged joy.

A full-figured woman, with a full smile, authentically saying "Yes" to herself.

I could see why the photographer shot it. I could see why she chose to post it in her album. Which made me look at who the photographer was. My dear friend Whitney Brewer.

The image spoke to me because it's a reflection of conversations I've been having with women lately. Holiday food has been good and clothes aren't fitting the same. Women of all body types have been talking to me about weight.

So, I use this image to say to all women. "Say yes to yourself, as you are. Start from there and create an upstaged moment of joy." It's a good look on you.

January 2, 2021 - The End

He was placed in her life for a very specific purpose...to show her that love wasn't a task of labor. She was under the assumption that love required sacrifice and struggle.

He loved her without effort. So effortlessly that she couldn't respect it as love. It was too easy for him to make her feel it. There had to be a reason. He had to be up to something.

Her suspicions kicked in.

She placed him in a category that painted him as someone who was out to do her harm. All along he was simply trying to show her a different way of thinking... a different way of being. But she wasn't receptive. She had to figure him out, but he possessed no mystery.

He wasn't looking for anything from her, he was simply looking within her. That made her uncomfortable. No one had taken time to see her for who she was and embraced her on that merit. She always had to be something, do something, or change something.

He embraced her for who she was, but she hadn't fully embraced herself, so his embrace was impossible.

The end.

January 8, 2021 - Lies

I wish that you had a reference for me in your history of men. I have known women like you but you have never known a man like me. I'm not saying that you're average. I'm just saying that I'm different. Not special. Just different.

On my journey I have encountered Truth, and when you have found Truth, you lose a taste for lies. Santa Claus is a lie. No matter how much society romanticizes the idea...it's a lie.

The same with love... The things you find worthy of celebrating in love are lies. Just because society collectively agrees doesn't make it right, or righteous. Monogamy for instance. A commonly known reason to celebrate love. I know a self-proclaimed cereal monogamous woman who recently divorced her husband for cheating. At the end, she held a bag of resentments, telling me about all the men she could've given a chance over the years. Such logic has never made sense to me. Repression of natural, human, connection doesn't make sense to me. Nor does the assumption that all connections lead to sex.

We all have gifts that nurture the evolution of humanity. Everyone has a testimony. Everyone has something that God gave them to give away. To think that these gifts are given to fit into the context of a single relationship is utterly ridiculous. Lies.

January 9, 2021 - Bittersweet

Sometimes "self-love" can be a bittersweet reality. I think all conscious people have moments when they want to be normal. Consciousness can be lonely. Sometimes I wish that I cared about someone's perception of me for the sake of human connection. Not liking me is a point of discourse. And with discourse comes understanding. I wish that I cared enough to understand why someone wouldn't like me.

But I'm conscious. I like myself so it doesn't matter what anyone thinks. In turn, I tend to attract people who share my consciousness. I have found that people who love themselves...love me. Automatically. We are the same person.

Recently, someone attacked my character and I smiled with no need to defend. Then I became sad. The sadness stemmed from witnessing someone attacking themselves.

The fight that she brought to me was a reflection of her own internal war.

Self-love is a guardian of peace of mind, so even though I witnessed her conflict, I had no desire to participate. Sometimes it's painful to watch people hurting and possessing no desire to heal them.

Such a reality can be considered heartless or extremely mindful. Bittersweet.

January 9, 2021 - Side Guy

It requires a high degree of emotional intelligence to be a "side guy". Once she chooses you, your job is to monitor her posts and watch for signs of turbulence. Don't bother her phone and burden her with the need to communicate. Your job is to pay attention. That's the agreement. She hires you to pay attention.

If you aren't Facebook friends, still... pay attention. That 'out of the blue' text isn't an accident. It's a call for help. It's her way of saying "I need you. Be on standby."

Your job is to carve out space for her to breathe. To accomplish this, you must be in-tuned with the divine feminine. You must know when she needs to vent or gossip. You must understand when she needs you to ravish her and blow her mind. Sometimes sex is just a naked conversation. During those conversations listen attentively. And if she asks your opinion, never speak against her man. After all, she chose him. Support her choice.

Position yourself to remove her guilt and self-doubt. Your job is to support, uplift, and please. Period.

And this...requires a high degree of emotional intelligence.

January 10, 2021 - Petty

He sat in her inbox for three months. Unread.

Then it happened... She became bored with her public page and ventured into her inbox.

There he was. The same guy who had been chiming in on her posts. She remembered him because, recently, she had proudly updated her profile picture and it only had a few likes. He gave it a heart and a pleasant compliment. He became "The new guy" on her radar.

She saw that his message was three months old. It didn't need to be opened. You could read it without clicking it.

A simple sentence...a date and time for dinner.

A statement of fact, not a request.

"The balls of this guy!" she laughed yet still opening it so that he could see that she had.

She was expecting him to instantly follow up since she opened the door. A week went by before she got a message. "How rude." This led to a communication exchange about manners. She thought it was cute. Being schooled by an old school gentleman. "He's funny!" After a few exchanges she asked, "Why haven't you asked me out again since we're talking now?"

"Because I'm a gentleman." He responded.

"What does that mean?" She asked in confusion.

He continued..."I wanted to take you out three months ago. Sincerely. At this point, if I took you out it would just be a game. I'd show you the time of your life only to ghost you. I'm a gentleman but I have the tendency to be petty."

January 10, 2021

She was tired of being tired. The typical empath who feels everything too deeply...

Sees everything too clearly. Painfully aware of life. Sometimes it was just too much.

Life/death. Love/hate. Man/woman.

Darkness/light. She felt everything so deeply that the dualities of life felt like a crossroads in her soul.

Why did she have to choose a side... a way? Why was choice even necessary? Why couldn't life be life, and God be good...always? Why couldn't reality be consistent?

These questions became meditations. She was the type of woman to seek desolate spaces to ponder life. Spaces that were once beautiful, now abandoned. Sort of like her.

Even without decor and maintenance, the raw bones of the structure possessed an aesthetic of its own. The space was a reflection of her. Abandoned and unkept yet sustaining a sense of beauty. Who was she to refuse the background which also served as a reflection?

No one.

She was no one, and everyone, in the same breath. And in that breath, she struggled the find reasons to keep breathing.

January 11, 2021 - Therapy

She said "You're one of the kindest men I've ever met. How can you be so callus?"

"I was born into a family that was already established. I had two siblings that were ten years older than me. Their dad died and my dad helped raise them once he hooked up with my mom. They didn't like my dad. For good reason, I guess. I've heard stories. Doesn't matter. My point is...this was the context I was born in. If they didn't like my dad, how do you think they felt about me? My mom left my dad when I was 5. It was normal not to have him around. I didn't realize the need of having a dad until I was 12. I started hustling. That's when I recognized a need for guidance so I looked up to the OG's. They had the game. The game led me to prison when I turned 18. I was sentenced to life. My homies signed statements against me. Another one of my homies got my girlfriend pregnant."

She said "Damn, I can see why you're so callus and distrusting."

I'm not distrusting. In fact, I'm extremely trusting. I trust people to be, exactly, who they are. The problem is...they don't know who they are and I no longer have an interest in trying to figure them out.

January 13, 2021 - Before

BEFORE you can expect him to understand your feelings you must make sure that he's capable of feeling. Then you must understand his emotional motivation. Does he like you because he wants to have sex with you? Does he like you because wants to take you off the market? Does he like you because he sees you as a potential wife? Your responsibility is to identify his emotional motivation.

BEFORE you can expect him to treat you as a value, you must make sure that he can recognize a value. Does he possess values? Does he have a healthy relationship with his mother? What did she teach him about women? Ultimately, you will be treated according to his conditioning. If he has a low esteem of women, you can't exceed his perception or raise his standards.

BEFORE you can expect someone to love you the way you want to be loved, you must first love yourself.

BE FOR self BEFORE anything else.

January 16, 2021 - Farewell

She paid him for an hour session and after five minutes into the conversation he returned her deposit. "This is a waste of time. I can't possibly charge you because I can't help you."

She asked "What do you mean? You helped Kim, so I know you can help me."

He responded "Kim is sane. You're not. You need therapy, not counseling."

"How can you claim to be a healer and speak in such terms!?" She exclaimed.

"Madam, I've never claimed to be a healer. I'm an advocate of common sense.

I simply asked you why you chose to stay with him if all you do is complain about his behavior. Your response... 'Because I love him.'

"I'm not judging you. But I'm not the guy for you. I can't take your money in clear conscience. You want to be sold a dream. I'm a realist. I'm not a dream seller. My knowledge doesn't apply to people who value fairytale over fact. Your dilemma is simple. You complain about his behavior because you're a 'complainer' and he mirrors your need to complain. That's the source of your issue. That's the function of your dysfunction; thus it becomes a choice.

But you love him so there is nothing a rational person could say to you to change your mind or shift your thinking. With that said... I bid you a peaceful farewell."

January 18, 2021 - Boss Lady

You can recognize her by her posts. She's the "all or nothing" type. Unwilling to settle.

She has high standards. She values consistency. And when she lets you in, she'll lift you up.

This is why she hurt so deeply. Every time she had given her all to a man, she ended up let down. In the worst way.

The higher the standard the greater the disappointment.

Her self-esteem was such that it was hard for her to understand how a man could fumble her loyalty. She was certain that she was a prize. Worth keeping, protecting, and upholding.

She only wanted the same effort she gave. It was simple. Not too much to ask. Her standards became her cross. A subconscious burden in the form of a statement.

"I don't need a man. I'm just fine by myself. No drama and I'm successful." Relentless drive covers her heartache. Emotionally intelligent, financially literate, socially stable, and upwardly mobile. A man would be a fool not to want her.

Due to her beauty and stature, she was skilled at deflecting men's advances. She wasn't looking for anything. She didn't have time to play games. The game she was playing involved expanding her personal empire.

Everyone asked her, "Why don't you have a man?" She hated that question. It implied that something was wrong with her. She'd offer a polite response, but in her mind she thought, "Bitch, I'm not looking for a man. I'm created for a boss!"

January 18, 2021

Her boldness was undeniable. She stood in the proud strength of self-awareness. Her journey to self was filled with darkness. A darkness she had grown to embrace as a personal truth. She naturally stood out because she overstood the things she had overcome. She walked in power, not fear. This brought her, both, adoration and envy. She didn't mind. She was convinced of who she was.

Empowered to see "past" anyone who cared to misunderstand her, and "through" anyone who cared to offend her. She was a bulletproof blend of hip hop and rock n roll. A paradox.

A tree...rooted in darkness with branches of enlightenment. She understood the superiority of nature, which made her a vehicle of the supernatural. Yes, she could cast spells. Yes, she had a direct line of communication to the spirit world. But her particular magic was rooted in her unapologetic individuality. Effortless charm with no intent to harm. But people are so insecure that sometimes her boldness could be offensive.

Fuck 'em.

January 19, 2021 - Yes

They tried to get it out of their systems but it still remained. A passion of toxicity.

Being on the brink of letting go, then crashing into each other violently naked.

Make up sex. Fucking to make a statement. Cocreating a moment of exclusivity.

No love. Unable to trust feelings. Only needing to trust bodies.

Scent marking and clawing. The familiar agreement of raw pleasure.

The beauty of make-up sex is that it's about vulnerability. Pure vulnerability.

Both parties giving up their need to fight, submitting to a moment of YES.

January 23, 2021 - Take Care

If a man fears another man in relation to a woman, it's because he isn't the man he thinks he is. If he fears that she will cheat, he isn't taking care of her body. If he fears another man's conversation, he isn't taking care of her mind. If he fears that she will develop feelings for another man, he isn't taking care of her heart.

He who takes care, loves without fear.

Take care.

January 23, 2021 - Haters

Prison teaches you invaluable lessons about human character and energy. To navigate the experience, you quickly learn that you can't fight your way out of every situation. An evolution of consciousness occurs. The inmate evolves into the convict. The convict knows how to deal with negative people energetically.

Prison is a tribal and primitive environment. The strong over the weak. To acquire strength most people join tribes (gangs). They move in packs. Then there's the individuals who move by themselves. Their strength resides within.

On my journey, the more power I gained the more hate I inspired. I've come to understand that power is the root of all of my conflicts. A hater is the opposite of lover. Self-love makes people attack you. Mainly people that are close to you. They start out saying things like "You're full of yourself." or "You act like you're all that."

I'd argue that the prison experience is more intense than society because you're around people who have nothing to lose. Strength is the primary currency. Everyone is on the same playing field. The rich dad can't pass down strength to his son. There is no inequality in prison. The inequality comes into play when a man evolves into power. The powerless look at you as if you've done something wrong and further seek to punish you for it.

January 23, 2021

She wore her blackness as a badge of honor. It wasn't enough to be beautiful, sleek, and toned. It wasn't enough to be elegant, poised, and graceful. She made a statement in whatever she did and whatever she wore.

Overachievement was a staple of her character.

The struggle forced her to go beyond the call of duty in all affairs. But her shoe selection was the exclamation point of her presence and mood. You could judge her mind state by what she stood on. When she summoned her fierce stilettos, she was intentionally rising above the bullshit. Putting her foot in the game, establishing a force field against the lame. You couldn't "Hey baby" her into a conversation. You had to come correct.

Bathsheba. She was the woman King David killed for.

David wasn't playing. Neither was she.

January 27, 2021 - Jody

He told me that he was in an open relationship. His lover was going to see another man in a different state. He had an issue with it. I asked him why. He said that she brought the conversation to him after the fact. She had chosen to go visit the guy without consulting with him. I asked, "Why does it matter if you're in an open relationship?" He said it was a matter of respect. She had decided to go visit the guy without consulting with him. I asked him if he had ever done the same thing. He said yes, with a "but" behind it.

I responded "She's following your lead. She's mirroring your behavior. The moon reflects the sun." He wasn't prepared to hear that. He shook his head in silence.

I passed him the weed and filled his glass with bourbon.

It's Jody's turn, Bruh.

January 28, 2021 - God-Fearing

We are direct reflections of each other... Spiritual contradictions. If we both believed in God the way we claim, we would not be in this stale mate. God is Love and we are created in His image. So, if we are love, we should be "in" love.

We should be sharing the same atmosphere of love. But we are not. We are both possessed by the demon of fear. It holds us back from serving Gods will.

The love inside of me creates fear inside of you. The love inside of you creates fear inside of me. But the beauty of it is that I am not prone to be afraid. So, you give me the opportunity to look at my reflection and question what I see. Empowering me to ask, "Why am I afraid?"

Allowing me to answer myself honestly. "I'm afraid because I am God fearing..." After all, God is Love.

February 3, 2021 - Hand in Hand

She told him that they could have great sex without connection. "Everything doesn't have to be about love and spirituality."

He disagreed.

"There can be no sex without connection, and everything is spiritual. When your spirit is low, you feel sad. When your spirit is high, you feel happy. Spirit and experience go hand in hand. The highest form of happiness is pleasure. Nothing is more satisfying than practicing pleasure with someone you love. I empathize with your limited perception of sex. Before I explore the place where you give birth, I want to understand the things that gave birth to you."

"For me, sex happens way before the bodies touch. And it's not about penetration. Sometimes sex is found in a naked embrace. Simply being present. Breathing each other in silence. Sometimes intimacy trumps raw passion. The love and connection is shaped by the spirit of the moment. They all go hand in hand."

February 4, 2021

She said, "A real man only needs one woman."

Where did you learn that? Why do you think that? If what you say is true then God would've made one woman for each man and the divorce wouldn't be higher than the success rate.

Truth is... A real man can have as many women as he can afford. It's a numbers game. There is no mystery about it. A man of value has choices.

She said, "We have choices too!"

I totally agree, but you are choosing to believe that a real man is defined by his ability to sacrifice his power of choice. That's why you are alone. That's why you pride yourself on not needing a man. Your independence has made you masculine. I see why it's hard for you to attract the man you claim to want.

She said "Oh I can be feminine and submissive for the right guy! But he has to show me that he's worth it." If your femininity is something that has to be unlocked, that means you show up to the table masculine. I bet your best friend is probably gay. She said, "He is, ironically, how did you know!?"

Because a masculine woman is prone to attract a feminine man.

February 6, 2021 - Dilemma

Baby, I understand your dilemma. You were designed to love me, and I was designed to love life. You want me to love you the same way I love life. But, in my mind, there is no contradiction. In loving my life, I love you, as you are a part of my life. But you need me to reflect your ex-husband. You want me to claim you. Separating you from the rest. Blinded you with a legal contract.

That's not how I work.

The contract is spiritual. It's energetic. We are not looking to create a family and join finances for a common goal. We are adults living life. I went to prison. You got married. But we both end up in the same place.

We are the same conversation in different words. You are fascinated by our attraction. I find it predictable. You loved me when you met me because I love myself. I would not waste my time on something that's not me. Love is the only result of my interactions. I'm narcissistic in that way. You wanted to know what this attraction was. You found out what it is. Now you're confused because you're trying to integrate me into an understanding that doesn't exist. Your reference for love is your ex-husband.

I understand your dilemma.

February 6, 2021 - Life

Relationships are like life. No one knows when it will end. The goal is to enjoy what you have while you have it. Period. There are so many damaged people in the world. So many people suffer from emotional hangovers. Intoxicated by failed romance. Holding the current lover to the mirror of the past.

I'm thankful for the time I served in prison. It gave me a deep appreciation for freedom.
It gave me an unwavering perspective on what life is about. I wake up and give thanks.

I practice being a blessing. It's a lifestyle. I look for ways to matter. I seek out spaces where my gifts make a difference.

Relationships are like life. Love is a democracy governed by capitalism. We chose who we love and how we love them. Most people hold back and limit their ability to profit from investment. People with wealth have a history of suffering great loses. For losing builds character, and character builds monuments. Be monumental in your relationships as you are in life.

Feb 24, 2021 - Real

Their relationship worked because it was real.

A real-ationship. They were on borrowed time.

Knowing that the future was an illusion they gave themselves to the moment...the real.

She wasn't looking for him. He simply arrived. A product of manifestation. An external reflection of an internal wish that she lacked the words to describe.

How do you ask the Universe for a paradox? What do you call a male unicorn? She couldn't have scripted a more perfect union.

Her life was in a transition from prison (marriage) to freedom. She didn't know what she wanted in a relationship. It wasn't a thought, consideration, or expectation. She was living her best life. Selfishly. Mindfully exploring all the things she had been denied as a ward of the state. Her life didn't have rules. She was an emotional anarchist - just like him.

A mutual belief in individual freedom held them in common. Making them more comrades than domestic partners.

That's why they worked...

Real talk.

February 21, 2021 - Breathe

She was so used to providing everything that she lost touch with Nothing.

Nothing was the space where her individuality existed. Nothing is where she was everything.

No-thing. Not an object. Pure, feminine, energy.

For her husband, and later, her children...she had to be everything. Her role as wife and mother consumed her sense of self. Her essence was lost to a manufactured identity. Social perception became an ever-present judge. God of her relationship.

Reality lost meaning. Life, like love, became a game of appearances. A grind to uphold an image of an unrealistic expectation.

What good is being everything to everyone but nothing to yourself? A battery without a charge has no value and a marriage that sucks the life out of you creates an atmosphere where divorce is a breath of fresh air.

Breathe...

February 25, 2021 - Polytics

She said "I don't understand all of that polyamory stuff. I'm not sharing my man."

He said "We have two points to address. First, your lack of poly understanding. Let's look at it like politics. If polyamory is a liberal democrat and monogamy is a conservative republican, I'm neither. I'd be an independent. Which I am. A self-governed thinker. I understand how both systems function and I choose not to participate. I don't endorse either one.

My personal constitution is based on individual freedom and collective spirituality. I know that we are all one and I trust our ability to do right by each other. No woman has the right to tell me who I can, or cannot, love. No woman can dictate 'how' I love. Nor do I want that power over a woman. My wife has a distant crush in another state. He writes her, texts her, and gives her FaceTime calls. I don't do any of that. I take her for granted. I'm focused on my business. He serves his purpose. He excites her as a woman. I don't want to be the only man who makes her feel alive. Individual freedom. Collective spirituality.

Second point... You say that you're not sharing your man, yet you are single BY CHOICE.

Why? Because every man that you've been with has cheated. So, you may not understand polyamory, but you've definitely been poly amorous."

March 6, 2021 - Boots

He asked her when the last time was she fulfilled a fantasy. The question threw her off.

She deflected by posing the same question to him, affording her time to consider a thought she had never questioned. Who thinks about fulfilling fantasies?

In response, he told her a story about an escapade he had the day before where he played "girlfriend" with his wife. He did her makeup, exaggerated her smokey eye, and dressed her up. If her appearance had a description, it would be "Classy Dominatrix".

He took her to an upscale establishment and instructed her to sit alone at the bar. He came in an hour later pretending to be a stranger. He sat directly across from her. Within the hour someone had paid for her dinner and multiple drinks had been sent her way. She told the bartender to extend her drink credits to the gentleman across the bar as she cashed out.

Once they got home and closed the door his hand was around her neck, her leggings were bundled around her ankles.

"Keep the boots on..."

March 6, 2021 - Giving Up

You push me away only to pull me close. I let you go only to hold on. Toxic? Maybe.

The truth of who we are to each other can't be argued. I don't want to argue. I only want to spell out the truth. The only consistent reality between us is that we always come back together.

You are the most grounded woman I have ever met. Your convictions make up the substance of your character. Yet there is something about me in your veins. I'm a part of your DNA. But I'm an undomesticated man. I can't be tamed. You flaunt your convictions. You tell me that I knew what you wanted in a partner from the beginning. Yet, you knew I wasn't built for that role. Just as you were clear with me, I was clear with you. I don't do cages and locked doors. You know that which is why you justify your disposition against me. That's fine.

What you don't know is that I'm aware of the power of my seed. So, when you received me, I became planted in your spirit. You don't like that because you weren't prepared for it. You invited me to your bedroom out of curiosity. It was a social experiment. You manifested me at a time when you were vulnerable to masculine presence. If everything lined up according to your standards you'd give in. You gave in. There is no giving up.

March 11, 2021 - Dare

I dare you to text him that you need his mouth. I dare you to meet him in the bathroom for a quickie. I dare you to stop your busy day for a moment of passion with your person. And if you don't have a relationship where this is cool... I feel sorry for you. If you resent the idea of asking him for a spontaneous shot of head... My heart goes out to you.

What type of love is that? Look at all the thoughts that came with entertaining the very idea of asking. Even without sex being involved.

I hope that this conversation inspires you to bond. I hope the idea of random passion makes sense to your relationship. And if there is a blockage prohibiting you, at least, now you see it which makes you responsible to do something about it.

Life is far too short not to have fun with love.

I dare you.

March 14, 2021 - Choice

She said, "I love you."

He said, "I love you too."

She said "But you don't love me the same way I love you so I feel like I should walk away. I don't want to be hurt."

He didn't respond.

She said "See how easy it was for you to let me go? That's why I feel like I should walk away."

He said "You have the right to walk away. It's a choice. If I stopped you, I'd be infringing upon your freedom. Do you want to be loved or locked up?"

March 15, 2021 - Tipping

It was a form of sexual Kung fu called Tipping.

He mounted her with his morning erection and told her, "This is not about cumming...it's about connecting." She shook her head in agreement as he moisturized his tool with her folds. Slowly sliding up and down her entrance. Finally resting his tip on hers. Their most sensitive regions connected and she exhaled as their nerve endings amplified with increased awareness. She breathed into his mouth as his tongue mirrored the movement of his erection. Tipping hers.

His abs tightened as he arched his back to Tip her a lil deeper at a different angle. She became aware of her nipples rubbing against his coarse chest hair, which made her aware of her heart chakra. She confessed her love as she resisted the urge to have him all the way inside her. He held her body in place with a very controlled stroke. "It's not about the orgasm." She reminded herself.

As she relaxed into his flow, she felt the power of now. Her clitoris throbbed and stood erect as her pussy constricted on his bell head.

It was this moment that propelled him into another gear. Zero to sixty. He grabbed a hand full of her hip as his other hand grabbed her neck. She experienced his divine energy become savage. He fucked her through her orgasm, and into another, until he met her there...at the tip of the sexual experience. His roar filled the room, his seed filled her privacy.

Tipping.

March 17, 2021 - Football

She was losing sight of the game. The big picture. Like a quarterback who throws an interception in the first quarter and never recovers, she was doubting her ability to move the ball.

Relying on handoffs and short passes, her fear of making a mistake inspired the defense to be bolder in their blitz schemes. Her timidity was inviting pressure from the opposition.

She found herself frustrated with her offensive line, but she was really frustrated with herself for being afraid of making the big play. She scolded them in the huddle "Guys, you have to protect me!"

They scolded her in return "We can't protect you because you aren't protecting us. If you can't throw the deep ball they'll continue to rush extra men!"

March 28, 2021 - Childish

Sometimes adults are like children. The little boy who likes a girl will pull her hair. It's a show of aggression that symbolizes a feeling of affection.

Sometimes women will hurt you to say they love you. They'll push you away out of uncertainty or insecurity.

Such instances separate men from boys. The boy will take her actions personally. He will feel rejected and flee. The man will evaluate her motives and connect with her intention. He will understand that her pushing him away is a request for him to hold on. It's what I call Emotional Dyslexia. A form of reverse loving.

Every queen possesses an inner bitch. Every woman is a complicated product of this inevitable duality. The kings amongst men can handle her. Gracing her with the power of a consistent, absolute, presence. Holding space for her to be authentically true to the full range of her emotions. The good and the bad.

Kings understand how to match energy... how to become the lil boy who pulls hair as a show of affection.

March 29, 2021 - Opportunist

She described me as an opportunist. I couldn't tell if it was an insult or a compliment. Either way, it was a teachable moment.

I spoke to her about nature. How everything is connected. How the seed needs the soil, water, air, and the sun. It uses all these elements for the opportunity of growth.

Humans are no different. When a man chooses a wife, it's based on her ability to produce. The wife affords him the opportunity to create children and build a family. In society we spend the most time with people that allow us to capitalize. We give labor for profit. Across the board.

We don't have friends that are useless. A worthless person can't support growth. People who lack resources can't build anything.

So, hell yeah... I'm an opportunist. To the point, I can take your judgment and create an opportunity for understanding.

April 17, 2021 - Irreplaceable

When you pay attention to your reality you notice certain trends.

They say that we attract what we are. I've noticed that I have a thing for irreplaceable women. My feminine tribe is filled with unicorns. Every woman in my life possesses magic.

Yesterday I had a moment of vulnerability and wrote a love letter to my beloved. I broke down why she was special. It felt good to share something so intimate. Then I randomly decided to visit my favorite bartender.

She's magical. The way she navigates men and manages her space. She's intuitive and attentive. She looked me in my eyes, connected with my soul, and asked me a very pointed question about my life. Her question touched directly upon something that is missing. I could see her wheels turning, plotting ways to support me manifest my vision.

I went to visit my therapist. Her magic is found in her ability to still my consciousness. Her kisses exude Zen. Her connection to me connects me to God. She's an experience not a conversation.

Every woman in my life is uniquely designed with an irreplaceable nature.

To think... We attract what we are. Irreplaceable…

April 18, 2021 - Self Love

I had a moment of clarity where I saw God as Self Love.

We say that God is all present, all knowing, and all powerful. We know that energy and matter can't be created nor destroyed. So everything in existence has always been here.

The ancestors tell a story about creation. "Consciousness became conscious of being conscious, and creation became a means for consciousness to experience itself."

It reminds me of the Self Love narrative. People who love themselves find great pleasure in sharing that love. They look for ways to be a blessing. A lack of expression equals death.

Life, itself, is a movement of creation. If something isn't growing it's dead.

Self-Love stimulates life. Lovers become magicians that make people feel alive. And what's the point in being alive if you don't feel it...Feel good. Feel God.

April 26, 2021, Out of the Blue

He was experiencing a disconnect in his marriage. Their love had become a chore. A routine.

He wanted to reignite the passion they once shared. I asked him if he knew what type of porn she liked. He didn't. That became his homework.

He returned and told me that she liked "girl on girl" porn. He seemed surprised because she's not bisexual. That was the source of his problem. He lacked imagination.

Homework...watch lesbian porn for a week.

He returned. I asked him if he saw a common thread in the various scenes. "Yes." he responded "They were all extremely sensual. Like, passionate and erotic mixed." "What does that tell you?" I asked. He seemed puzzled.

His conclusion: Maybe she was secretly bisexual. I couldn't hold back my laughter. I asked him if he was in touch with his feminine side. He told me that he didn't have one.

And pretty soon, buddy... you won't have a wife.

April 30, 2021 - Upset

When a woman is upset, she is both Up and Set. She's above her range of operation (Up) and (Set) in her ways. A bird can't fly sitting down, thus her frustration. She knows that she is built for more but she doesn't know how to achieve it. She knows that she deserves a higher status but she doesn't know how to acquire it.

A woman who is upset is a confused bird. Her instincts tell her that she has the capacity to fly but her conditioning holds her down. She gets comfortable in sitting. Then she takes pride in walking. Just getting by. Surviving. But the sky communicates directly to her soul. Nothing is more painful than possessing the ability to fly but lacking how. Which is why she's upset.

May 2, 2021 - Holistic Love

It wasn't just sex with him. It was a blend of yoga, meditation, prayer, and rhythm. It involved stretching, conscious breathing, thanksgiving, and dance. More than sex it was a practice of physical oneness. A release exercise.

Individual "I's" letting go to become We.

She came to him, for him, on him. He probed her for understanding. Discovering spaces that made her say "Yes!" He gave himself to her arrival. Once she came, his animal disappeared. Morphing into a lesbian. Intense thrusts transformed into tender kisses. His hands caressed her body as divine art. Her mouth became the focus of his sexual energy as he lay buried inside of her. The walls of her yoni applauded his erection as she struggled to gain her breath. He made love to her mouth with his tongue. They lost themselves in the collective sensation of being One.

More than sex... holistic love.

May 6, 2021 - She Sighed

She sighed...

She confessed that she had developed feelings for him and asked him his thoughts.

He responded "You haven't developed feelings. The feelings were already there. I am simply a manifestation of feelings that already existed."

She accused him of being philosophical to evade the point.

"The point is you! I spoke about you and your feelings. I told you that I was a manifestation of those feelings. How did I evade the point?"

She sighed.

He continued "Allow me to ask... What did you want in your life when you met me?"

She said that she just wanted someone to have fun with. Someone to love on her terms. Deep conversations, great sex, live bands and dance floors. She wanted someone to be free with.

"Am I that? A manifestation of a feeling you had before I ever came in the picture?"

She sighed...

May 6, 2021 - Alchemy

He could feel her pulling away. Her complaints against him were becoming repetitive. She was growing tired of arguing and trying to pull away. Other men willingly gave her the attention that she so desired from him. She was beginning to weigh her options.

But he understood the scales of justice. He understood that she would never pour into another man what she had poured into him. It takes too much time to establish the level of trust they shared. It wasn't worth the effort.

So, as a good steward of love, he transformed the energy of her tantrums. He consciously argued with her to make sure she exhausted her frustrations. He took them in and held them for later.

Later was always in the bedroom...where he would aggressively feed her the violence she had given him. This was his way of saying "I love you... All of you."

Alchemy.

May 14, 2021 - SuperNatural

She asked him if he believed in the supernatural. He confirmed.

"Good" she said, "because I like you and I'm going to explore what it feels like to love you. I'm going to be everything you need, then I will disappear. Can you handle that without your feelings getting involved?"

"Absolutely!" he responded with laughter.

"Why are you laughing? I'm serious!" she interjected.

"I'm laughing because I'm rejoicing. I can't take you for granted so each moment with you will hold the potential to become a beautiful memory. Each kiss, every hug, will be conscious. Can you imagine having sex like it's going to be the last time. The urgency of the passion. The freedom of the sexual imagination. So yes, I laugh because I rejoice. When you choose to disappear, I will disappear with you because I will be inside of you. The question becomes...can you handle that without your feelings getting involved?"

May 14,2021 - Bar-tend-her

She randomly asked him who he was and it threw him off...

She had been waiting to approach him. He was a new face at a local bar but there was nothing 'local' about him. She was the managing bartender. Good at reading clients but perplexed by his demeanor.

She asked "Who are you? I can't figure you out. When you first came here, I thought you were law enforcement. Then I thought, maybe a preacher. But you ordered a double shot of bourbon and had an exotic, dark, beer. Police and preachers don't drink like that."

She continued..."and everyone seems to like you. Even the people who don't like people. You have a way about you. Who are you?"

He just smiled.

She continued..."I thought you were a player because I always see you with beautiful women but I've overheard your conversations. You're more the inspirational type. You wear a ring but I know you're not married. So what's up with you? Who are you? What do you do for a living?"

He smiled at her observation and responded,

"I'm just a man living life to the fullest."

May 19.2021 - Static

The beauty of the prison experience is that it teaches you how to love without attachment.

I see people out here struggling to grasp this concept. Suffering because they associate love with possession. In prison, receiving mail from women sustains your sanity and keeps you connected to the real world. No righteous convict would depend on "one" woman for all his incoming mail.

He wouldn't burden her with that responsibility. You never want to run the risk of burning someone out. So you outsource your need for connection. You build a team of loyal friends and spread the responsibility amongst them. It works. No single person feels like they are carrying a load, so the connections last longer. If one falls off, it simply opens space for another connection.

Social relationships are the same. I can love you deeply and not take you personally. My love isn't static. It's fluid. It assumes the position of its host.

This can be a good thing or a bad thing depending on who's involved.

The woman who accepts me as fluid can flow with me.

The woman who expects me to be static, fixed, contained...

Well, that causes static.

May 23, 2021 - Baffled

He suffered from the "good guy" complex and lost a good woman because of it.

I explained to him that to keep her he needed to speak her language. I determined her language by the duration of her longest relationship. She was married 12 years to a man who ruled with an iron fist. Understanding this, he proceeded to love her in a way that she wasn't used to. He didn't try to control her. He placed no demands on her. He was supportive of her decisions until she decided not to see him anymore.

Baffled. He explained how he thought things were going good for them.

I explained that if she endured 12 years with a mean spirit, being a good guy was the wrong approach.

Baffled. He asked what I meant.

I explained... If a woman would stay married to a man who raises his voice how could she stay connected to a soft-spoken gentleman. That's obviously not a language she speaks or respects, which is why you lost her.

Baffled.

May 23, 2021 - Dance

It was all playful fun until a certain song came on. Then the living room became a dance floor.

One woman started twerking and flexing her hip control. He acknowledged her skill and looked back to the TV. The song had a video he had never seen. She started gyrating harder to attract his attention. He kept looking at the video.

The other woman broke out in dance and shifted the energy of the room. He found himself in a trance. Unlike her friend, she wasn't begging for attention. She commanded it.

He found himself studying her. Her body became magnetic. A dark, sensual, energy radiated from her eyes. She moved like a serpent goddess. He felt compelled to move with her. A burst of oxytocin was released from his brain combined with a sense of lust. He craved her in a non-sexual way that was intensely sexual. It wasn't about being inside of her, it was about being with her...around her. He wanted to groove with her. Hold her. Become one with her rhythm. He wanted to fuck her with clothes on to a trap song.

Dance.

May 25, 2021 - Fake Love

He summarized his failed romance with negative emotion. He said it was "fake love".

I challenged his observation. "Why do you call it fake?"

He said, "Because if it was real she wouldn't have walked away from it."

He told me a story about trust issues and how she made him feel comfortable enough to let his guard down. Now he was negating the beauty of their entire connection by the outcome. Erasing a whole relationship because she moved on. I admit... I was a bit aggravated because it's hard for me to perceive love as fake. And it's hard for me to see grown men cry. I lost patience and ushered us to the bottom line. "In your honest heart, right now, what do you want for her... the best or the worst?" Without pause, he said "Nothing but the best!"

"Ok, so what if moving on was the best for her...would you be happy?"

"Of course!"

"So why are you sad?"

Him: Hits blunt. Shuts TFU.

May 29, 2021 - Imagine

She said "You're a fraud. You're pretending to be something you're not."

I said " You're correct. It works for me. I was once a child who thought I could do anything. I became a man who thinks the same. In prison, I imagined myself free until I manifested freedom. Living from my imagination works for me. It's a gift from God. Of course, you would perceive me as a fraud because I'm not attached to a certain identity or ideology.

I am that I am. I can move in any circle and not lose myself. I'm free. My imagination brought me through the worst form of human oppression and it will carry me to the highest version of my realized self."

Imagine that...

May 29, 2021 - Ripples

To them, making love was an intentional ritual. They would give themselves to each other for the sake of humanity. They would kiss and wish intimacy for their friends. They would become one flesh and wish pleasure for the world.

She would take his body and give hers for the taking. Every time.

It started when they first made love. She smiled and witnessed his body move. It seemed like a movie. He gave himself to her in a way that seemed to require lots of effort. She grew to understand that it was effortless. He wasn't "trying". He was going with the flow. It was here that she became aware of their rhythm. Their natural passion was like a song that forces you to dance. An effortless groove.

Every morning, they would create a tone for the day by making love. They would extend this tone to their immediate circle and to humanity. They called this practice "Ripples".

May 30, 2021 - Hints

We do this thing where we drop hints in our conversations. I hear you and I know that you hear me. We are trying to maintain boundaries, but we both want to push the limits as well. This is our form of fun. Life doesn't always present us with perfect storms. This is ours.

In my heart, I believe that we could handle the transgression. I believe that we could compartmentalize a night of passion. But I'd never let us go there. We already like each other too much for that to happen. We would only like each other more, and I'm not prepared to deal with that consequence. Right now, we have a safe space to love each other platonically. We support each other's interests as friends.

A night with you would be beautiful because I could express my gratitude for you in a different way. And knowing that it would just be a night, I would let loose. So would you.

That could be dangerous. Which is why it's so much fun to think about. However, out of my love for you, I will always protect the big picture. My urges will only live in my imagination. Our relationship will remain solid and unfuckwithable. I'd rather be the guy you count on than the guy you bounce on.

May 30, 2021 - Trigger

I'm growing to realize that there are some people in the world who look for reasons to be angry. They get offended if you don't wear a mask, take the vaccine, or anything that doesn't line up with their fear-based perception of what's right. There are people who will read thought provoking posts and not respond but see something that offends them and jump in the comments with all sorts of hostility. I used to think that this way of thinking was unique to prison because the environment is so negative. Inmates have a consistent reason to be upset. But you people are free. You are not confined. You have access to your children and family. You have jobs, cars, and houses. You have the choice to change jobs, vehicles, or neighborhoods. You have so much to be thankful for so it's hard for me to understand your choice to be so quick to resort to anger as your emotional response to life.

I wonder what it's like to love you. I wonder how your partner feels. I wonder if they walk on eggshells around you because you'll be triggered if they say the wrong thing.

June 1, 2021 - Witch Way

She sensed his internal discomfort through the phone. He didn't have to say anything. He wasn't good at talking about his problems. A bit of a loner.

"Let me see your face. Come over." she said.

He arrived at her house to a potion of essential oils, a fire pit, his favorite spirit, and her. Tanned white skin adorned in a lavender silk nighty. Her erect nipples shown through the fabric and clearly, she wore no panties. "Drink this and feel what you feel." He drank the potion and she placed a crystal around his neck. Escorting him to the fire she handed him a bottle of liquid.

"These are your negative feelings. Feel what you feel. Channel those feelings into this bottle and let's bid them farewell. I don't want to hear about it. Feel what you feel privately. Channel it here."

She handed him the bottle and began to prance around the fire until she danced in celebration. He followed instructions. "Pour them into the fire" she joyfully chanted.

Apparently the liquid inside the bottle was slightly flammable. As he poured it into the fire it erupted. She said "This fire is your appetite for life. All emotions contribute to it, even the negative. Rise king. Everything works towards your favor. Nothing holds you back."

He was pondering which way to go. He went the witches' way...

June 2, 2021 - Soul

You follow me but you don't acknowledge me. You like my work but you never express your approval. I used to wonder why. But after talking to you in person, I get it. You are concerned about what people think. My truth is edgy, like life. And when it resonates, you can't applaud. You must keep your position private. You are wise.

Thank you for in-boxing me and sharing your true self. I adore you for that, even though I don't agree with your concerns about public opinion. But I get it. You have to play the game.

I view you as a demographic. So I write this letter openly to thank you for your silent support and your resonation. Sometimes we all need to be reminded that we aren't alone. Especially when we challenge traditional values and social norms.

June 3, 2021 - Friends

Loving me will get you criticized. It will start with your friends. They will question your sanity. They will argue a strong case against me. I am part holy man and part villain. It's easy for people to find things not to like about me.

Our happiness will be demonized. Our natural chemistry will be annoying. Fresh romance is offensive to most people. Your friends aren't exempt.

We will dance to live music and they will think its raunchy. We will kiss 'out of the blue' and they will think it's unnecessary. It will appear that we are showing off. But really, we are just being authentic in our joy for each other and our mutual passion for life.

No one wants to see that shit.

So, keep me to yourself. Around your friends, let's just be friends. It's better that way.

Trust me.

June 3, 2021 - Dear Lord

Lord,

I want to thank you for prison. You forced me to interact and understand every type of asshole imaginable. You gave me armor and a word mightier than a sword. You gave me discipline and discernment. The ability to understand when to fight and the power to witness people fighting themselves without getting involved. You empowered me with an awareness of human nature. People pay thousands of dollars for a college that teaches them what you taught me through experience.

Thank you.

Because of you, I understand that "shit" is waste from the body that fertilizes the soil. So the shit I'm experiencing isn't a negative thing. It's waste from the body that fertilizes the soil. Assholes are necessary for this process to take place.

Let that shit go. Let that shit grow.

A mf'n MEN.

June 3.2021

Her beauty was hard to put into words...
She was a portrait of androgynous art. Her masculine and feminine were synonyms.

She was a gorgeous man in the form of a handsome woman. Her image alone would inspire you to stare. Secretly trying to figure out who she was. Knowing intuitively that she was someone. Her eyes, posture, and lips, spoke without saying a word. She was a powerful presence not just a captivating image. God created her to effect people in the deepest of ways. Her vibration was strong. Her soul was tender.

Rare.

She was the exotic seasonal flower that would come out to show love, only to meet the harsh elements of life. She celebrated the sunshine. She bathed in the moonlight.

She handled the storms, the rain, and the people who selfishly cut her from her roots to place her in a vase.

Her beauty was hard to put into words...

June 5, 2021 - Opinion

I had a heart-to-heart conversation with a dear friend. She's a business owner and entrepreneur. She expressed to me that she was tired of the grind. Burned out. Unmotivated to 'sale' herself and market her brand. She sighed "I just want a mindless job that pays decent."

It was hard for me to hear. Painful, in fact. She mentioned bartending and I became excited for her. My Gemini mind could see the connections of her gifts. Not only is she beautiful and good with people, but she's also a photographer. I imagined her serving drinks with her camera as a part of her attire. I coined the term "Brittany Shot" because everyone takes selfies at the bar when I'm out. Why not add the professional element to the night in the form of a $20 shot. ($8 for 2 shots + $2 gratuity + $10 for the picture.)

I could easily see the combination of her gifts creating a unique experience at someone's bar. I can't count the times I've asked a bartender to take a picture for me to capture a moment. But she couldn't hear me because I couldn't hear her. She was burned out. The idea of hustling was not what she wanted to hear. In fact, she didn't want to hear anything, she just needed to vent. Sometimes holding space for someone means holding back your opinion.

Lesson learned.

June 5, 2021 - Suffering

She said "What's wrong with him? He seems to enjoy watching me suffer?! And I keep going back for the same shit!!"

Perhaps you enjoy suffering. Why else return for more. He reflects something in you that, obviously, needs attention. So look at it. I hold no judgment about love styles. Some people have a flare for the dramatic when it comes to love. Some people like that sticky, possessive, love. I don't judge. I simply observe individual choice. You choose suffering, so I conclude that you like suffering. You can't blame him for making you suffer. You've accepted accountability for returning. Maybe if you stopped expecting him to change...you would change. But you don't want change because you like whips and chains. Nothing wrong with that either. As long as it's consensual. And your suffering is consensual.

I say, establish a "safe word" and have fun with it.

June 15, 2021

Everything costs. And valuable things require insurance.

The insurance on a healthy relationship is presence. Being fully present while you have it.

When it's gone there is no love loss because the love was inside each moment and each moment becomes a sacred memory.

-Sol Says...

June 21, 2022 - Muse

She laid naked in silence. Panting. Holding his hand. They stared at the ceiling as they caught their breath. She uttered "I wish you would use me as your muse. I'd love for you to describe this feeling. This peace. You totally clear my mind. Right now, I'm only conscious of how good my body feels. It's magical."

She continued, "I've never told you this, but I take medication for depression and anxiety. I've been weening myself off it and I've noticed that I never need it when I'm with you. Even if you're not here, the thought of you keeps me grounded. You're kinda like medicine. I'd love for you to write about this energy...this magic."

He responded "I write emotional fiction. Our love is the substance of a fairytale. We are adults living in our own imaginary world. No one would believe it if I wrote it. And we only believe it because we experience it."

She smiled in silent agreement.

January 25, 2022 - Dangerous

Out of the blue she said, "You're dangerous."

He laughed and requested an explanation.

"I love my husband, dearly, but you're the perfect man to cheat with. I know that I could let loose with you and there would be no judgment or receipts. You're a good-looking smooth-talker and your confidence intrigues me. That's dangerous. You carry a spirit of freedom and it makes me want to be free. Wild. Undomesticated. You know...just say fuck it and have some fun...some "Me Time."

"What does that look like for you?" he asked. Holding space for her truth.

"Good question. I'm not sure, but it feels erotic and forbidden. Wild and free. I don't feel a need to guard myself with you and who knows what could happen when there are no boundaries. That's scary."

"So, I'm not the one who is dangerous... It's you."

March 2, 2022 - Dear Yoni

Dear Yoni,

I wonder why they don't regard you as one of the nine Wonders of The World. After all, every human passes through you. You "re-create" man. If there is a connection between heaven and earth, the spiritual and the physical, surely it's you. To think, your purpose is to naturally perform miracles, so we take your power for granted. Even if you weren't gifted the ability to reproduce, you offer man the greatest pleasure on earth. Somehow, we don't see you for who you are. We don't celebrate you as divine. In fact, we do the opposite. We objectify you and oppress you. For this, I apologize.

I cringe when I hear men speak about you.

"I'm going to smash that."

"I'm going to beat that pussy up."

"I'm going to blow her back out."

Why? How did we grow to equate intimacy with violence. That violence translated into self-hatred. As a boy I was taught to repress my feminine side. Any of my peers who refused to fight would be called "pussy". Which caused me to become more violent. Which caused me to go to prison at a young age. Which caused me to tap into my feminine side. Which caused me to heal...become whole... Holy.

Thank you, Yoni.

April 13, 2022 - Femme Fatale (Painting)

She was a femme fatale. A highly attractive danger to men. She liked women too but with women she possessed a degree of empathy. With men, she was relentless. She had witnessed too much toxic masculinity. The darkest aspects of manhood. She had experienced and survived the unbelievable. "How could you do that to a child!" was a statement that unconsciously governed all her actions. Men were demons that needed to be tamed and punished for their transgressions. So, she became demonic to serve them justice. It wasn't a choice; it was a necessity. Her life was theatre. A cinematic blockbuster that featured a battle between darkness and light. It carefully, and very thoughtfully, played out how we are all complexed dualities. We are capable of doing the wrong thing for the right reason. Men had erased her sense of morality. She had become an addict of power. She was like a fisherman that does it for sport. Catch and release. Bait you, to catch you, to let you go. She was a sexualized tornado and men were her landscape. They were the terrain that gave her a reason for existing. Her internal rage needed an outlet.

Dark angel.

May 4, 2022 - Toxicity

Pardon my toxicity, but I love when you break up with me. I love when you make up your mind to end our relationship forcing me to miss you. It turns me on because I know that you miss me too. And we both know that it's only a matter of time before we reconnect. So until then I'll give you your distance. I'll agree to fall back and pretend that I don't love you. Or maybe my respect for your decision is, in fact, an act of love. Maybe I love you enough to let you go. Or perhaps I'm spiritual enough to faithfully practice nonattachment. However you frame it... It turns me on in a way that makes me feel alive. To know that you're going to open yourself to the next man in line. To know that your experience with him will only remind you of me. You'd attribute this to my ego. But I say its mathematics. Our connection is undeniable and indefinable. Which means we can't control it. You can only control things that have definitions. So good luck with your endeavor to place me in your past. I'm not capable of being confined by time or space. Our connection runs too deep. And the power of our privacy exceeds your will to let it go. I'll see you soon baby. And when I do... you know what it is.

~Toxic

May 16, 2022 - Gangsta

She was Gangsta. The type of woman who had been through enough shit to ask the right questions..."Is there anyone from your past that could show up and regain your heart?"

He thought about it and told her no. She said, "But who came to mind when you thought about it?"

He proceeded to speak candidly about an ex who was a unicorn. He appreciated his experience with her because it told him a lot about himself. It showed him his fears and limitations. She said "I can see your energy change when you speak of her. You still love her so I can never allow myself to completely love you. I wish I could, but I can't."

He responded "You already love me which is why we are having this conversation. You love me at the same time that I love her and there is no issue. What I feel for her is not taken from you. There is no loss on your behalf. Yet you are preparing yourself for loss in the future. So I'm glad we agree to pause our connection, because I couldn't move forward with a woman who's fear of loss is greater than her will to win."

He was Gangsta too.

June 10, 2022 - Gemini

You stimulate my Gemini. You make me want to bite and kiss softly. Choke and caress. Fuck and make love.

I imagine the things you've been through with men and I can't help the desire to show you something different. If only for 90 days. It will be a quarter of your year that you won't regret.

I see the wall that you've built around yourself. The fear disguised as boldness. Your beauty is a weapon. Love is war. That's why I want to make you naked and taste your core. Fuck that wall. It's meant to protect you. It serves no purpose if no one is trying to harm you. I come in peace. You sense that, which is why you've been so open thus far. You know that I see you because you want to be seen. Most men see your projection. I see your soul. That's a huge turn on for you. People like us need challenges. Stimulus with an element of danger. Life can become routine and I'm the guy to shake things up.

I'm man enough to be your lesbian. The girlfriend you can confide in. And black enough to take you into my masculine darkness safely. I'll hold your hand and guide you through a world that I fully understand. For, in darkness there is no sight. And without vision our other senses become more sensitive. That's why we smell each other like animals and kiss like we're hungry.

CONNECT WITH THE AUTHOR

TikTok: @spoken_sol
Email: solamenra@gmail.com

Spoken Sol

www.ingramcontent.com/pod-product-compliance
Ingram Content Group UK Ltd.
Pitfield, Milton Keynes, MK11 3LW, UK
UKHW021711190726
13853UKWH00001B/494